# Broken Footprints
# Faded Hearts

by
n.a.denmon

This book is drawn from a work of fiction. The characters, incidents, and dialogue are drawn from the author's imagination and are not to be construed as real. Any resemblance to actual events or persons, living or dead, is entirely coincidental.

BROKEN FOOTPRINTS FADED HEARTS. Copyright © 2018 by Nicholas Denmon. All rights reserved. Printed in the United States of America. No part of this book may be used or reproduced in any manner whatsoever without written permission except in the case of brief quotations embodied in critical articles and reviews. For information address D-Rated Novelists via Carlton Fields at Corporate Center Three, 4221 Boyscout Blvd, Tampa, FL 33607.

D-Rated Novelists books may be purchased for educational, business, or sales promotional use. For information, please email the Special Markets Department at CrossAtlanticAcquisitions@Gmail.com.

FIRST EDITION

Print & eBook Design by Glory ePublishing Services

Library of Congress Cataloging-in-Publication Data has been applied for.

ISBN 13: 978-1729873571
ISBN 10: 172987357X

## Also by Nicholas Denmon

### Fiction

For Nothing
Buffalo Soldiers
Ashes to Ashes (2019)

### Poetry

Broken Footprints Faded Hearts

### Join His Community of **Avid Readers**

**Facebook:** @nicholas.denmon
**Twitter:** @nicholasdenmon
**Instagram:** @nicholasdenmon
**Goodreads:** @Nicholas_Denmon

*To her, the she who taught me love.*

# Note to the Reader

Love each other. And from love, give the gift of empathy to those that you meet. The world is cold and callous enough as it is. The only way we add some light and warmth to this rock we call home, is to give a sense of understanding to those around us. We can warm one another by letting others know they are not alone. That we have shared and universal pains, problems, and concerns. If we start there, we will learn we can have the same joys, the same successes, and the same kinds of love.

Let empathy be the guiding light that calls each of us home.

*– n. a. denmon*

# Table of Contents

SHE ..................................................................1
ME ....................................................................53
THEM ..............................................................99
US .....................................................................147
About the Author ...........................................197

SHE is the first section of poetry and encapsulates my observations of many different women over the course of my life. It focuses on the trials of relationships, social and professional inequality, the pain caused from these cross sections of humanity, and invariably the strength that is developed when one undergoes the crucible of everyday life in our society.

• • •
Broken Footprints Faded Hearts

She hates to break

But cement cracks too

It lets the flowers through

•

She tried so hard to hear the
music, but it left her long ago.
Black watercolors fled in streaks
from eyes of melted hope. But for
her too, I can promise you, this
too will go. The music begins again
with first one heartbeat, then two,
you know. This swing of life is
never wrong, and soon true color
shall come back to hope. And the
beats, they'll drone on and on till
at last her song comes back in full

• • •
Broken Footprints Faded Hearts

•

She's finally realized what she's gotta do.

With sad eyes, she moves right through you.

There's a fire in her heart even you can't put out.

Call her crazy, but she knows what she's about and where you've ended was just supposed to be the start.

And lately, she's been the whole in a thing where she was promised to only play a part.

So, she's gotta do what a girl's gotta do, and she goes on.

This ain't nothing new.

Just now, it's without you

• • •
Broken Footprints Faded Hearts

•

Shattered girls

Once made of glass

Make weapons

Of their broken bits

You can't break a woman.
Women craft entire worlds from nothing.
You can only make her start again –
Without you

●

She's a survivor.

Scars are what happens

When you stop

Being a victim

・・・
Broken Footprints Faded Hearts

●

She felt tired before her time,

As if her body was born a century after her soul.

And every day since had been an endless game of tag

Against something too fast to ever catch

•

She became a conqueror

To take back the things

Stolen from her before

She ever took a breath.

Choice. Earning.

Sexuality. Equality.

Freedom.

It takes a warrior

To win a war

●

She always left a window open,
Knowing her blackbird might
One day fly away.
But it might just decide to stay
And learn home was never
Just some idea, didn't always
Have to be another day. Home
Could be right there with her,
And not all blackbirds need
Their cages anyway

It's a wonder

Watching her in her element.

She's just

Casually blowing minds

•

The woman in her knows

What the girl did not.

Love isn't just a word.

It's action.

Love shows up.

Being there matters.

If you want to be in her future,

You better be present today

●

If you don't know

Exactly what love is

She is the type of woman

That makes you

Want to find out

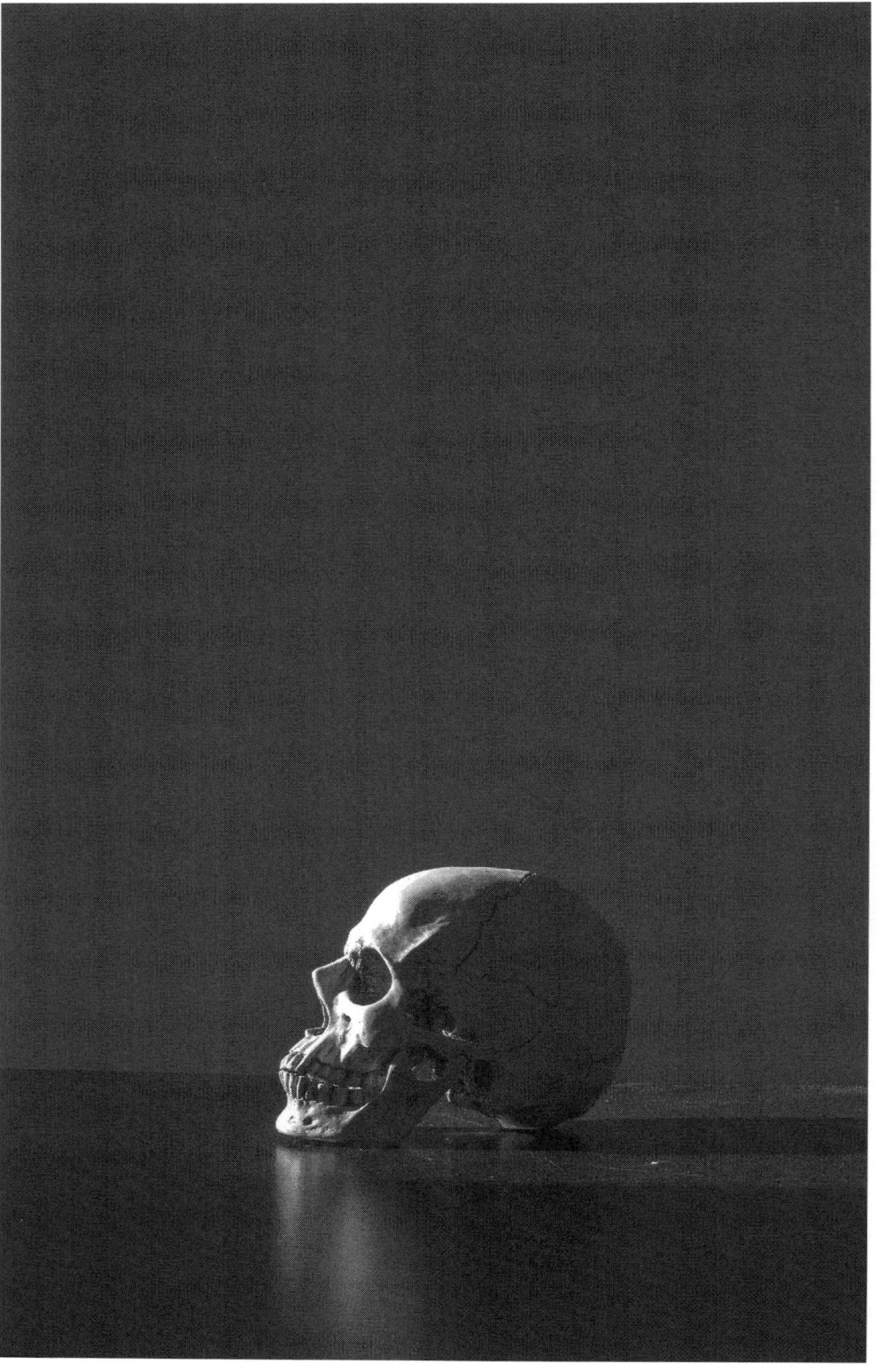

●

She was always a warrior.

She trained first against her mother,

The fiercest of her tribe

The warrior queen of her kin.

Then she battled him.

And the next him,

And him again.

Then she fought herself

For her self.

And she'll be damned if society

Thinks it gets to win.

Because she was born to fight,

And gladly will again

● ● ●
Broken Footprints Faded Hearts

●

She's beautiful because she's free

When you stumble upon a unicorn

You don't cut off her horn.

You just watch

And let her be

•

If only love came in a box, at least then she could feel its edges, smell the chocolate flavor of the cardboard, and gaze on it whenever she wished.

But it didn't.

Love came scattered on the back of an invisible hurricane and though she felt it, she could never catch it and she found its unpredictable nature unfair and undeserving.

But still, she kept jumping for it with greedy hands, growing always more tired, and leaping for smaller and smaller heights

• • •
Broken Footprints Faded Hearts

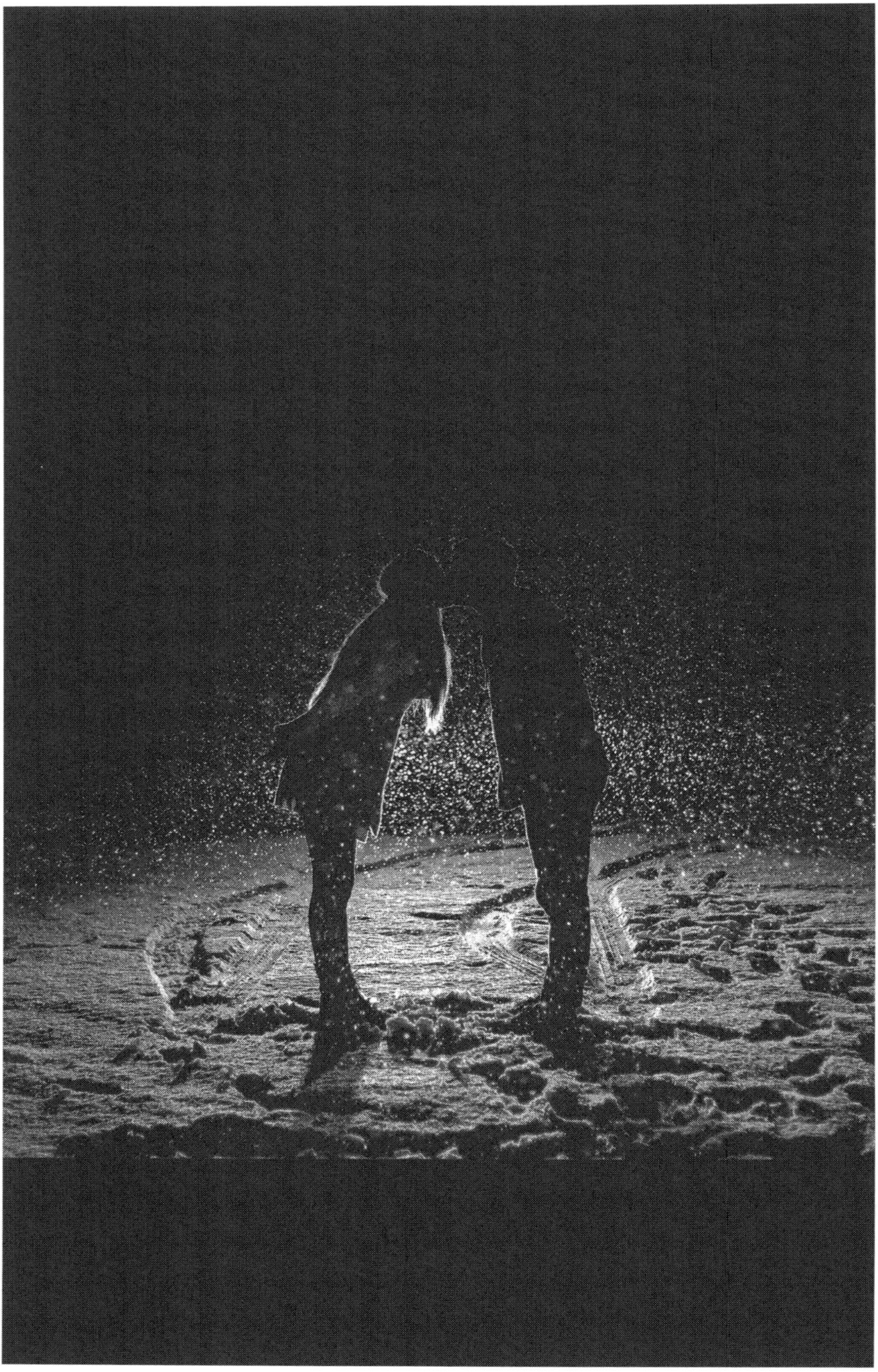

•

She loved like rain,

So vast

So shattered

And so heavenly

That it could reach him

Anywhere.

Some people wait for the rain,

Never knowing when the storm

Will break their way.

But with her

He was always soaked to the bone

As if it were April

Every day

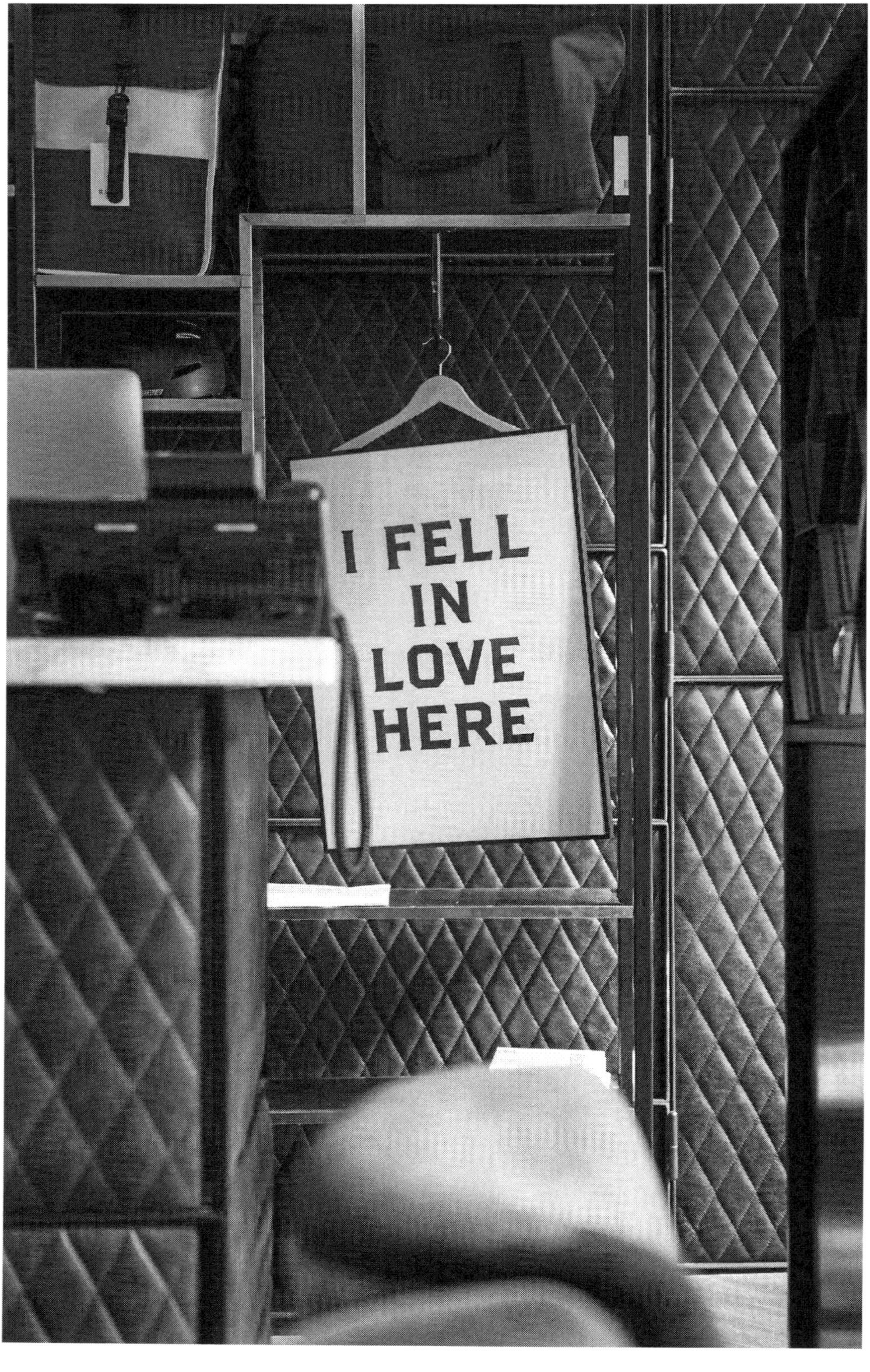
I FELL
IN
LOVE
HERE

•

She smelled of music

And spoke in watercolor

And I was disastrously

Drunk on

And acutely aware of

Everything

About her

She made her strength.

It wasn't given, but earned.

Shallow ones let her know how deep she went.

It was the cold ones that let her learn how hot her fire burned.

She is strong

From one thousand wrongs that helped to write

The woman's song.

All the words etched in stone, engraved upon a heart

She grew alone.

She's the woman

Made from the girl

They wish they'd known

Her smile bloomed

But once a year

And even then

Always in the dark

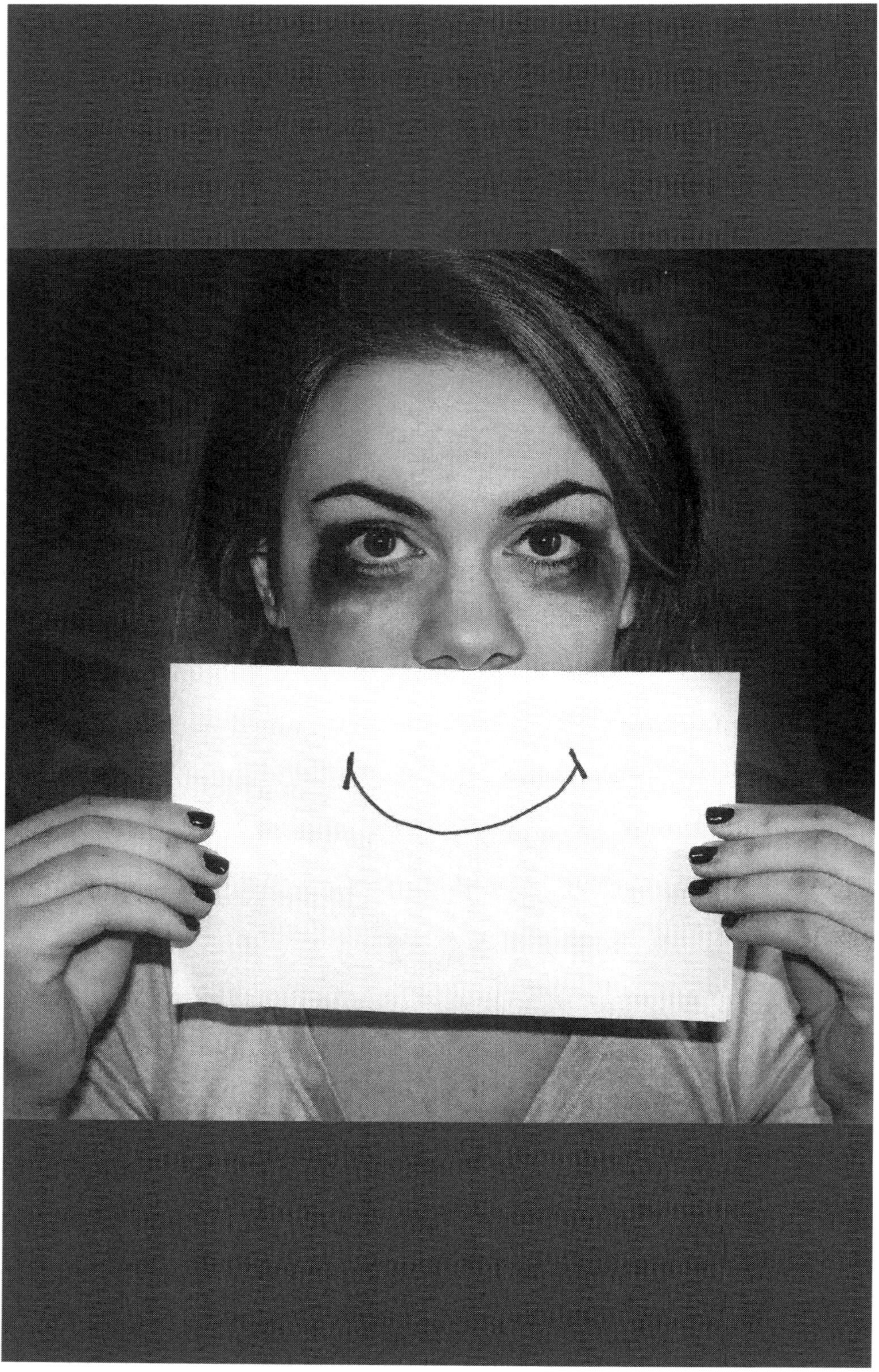

•

She hid the hurt

Beneath sad smiles,

Fooling only fools

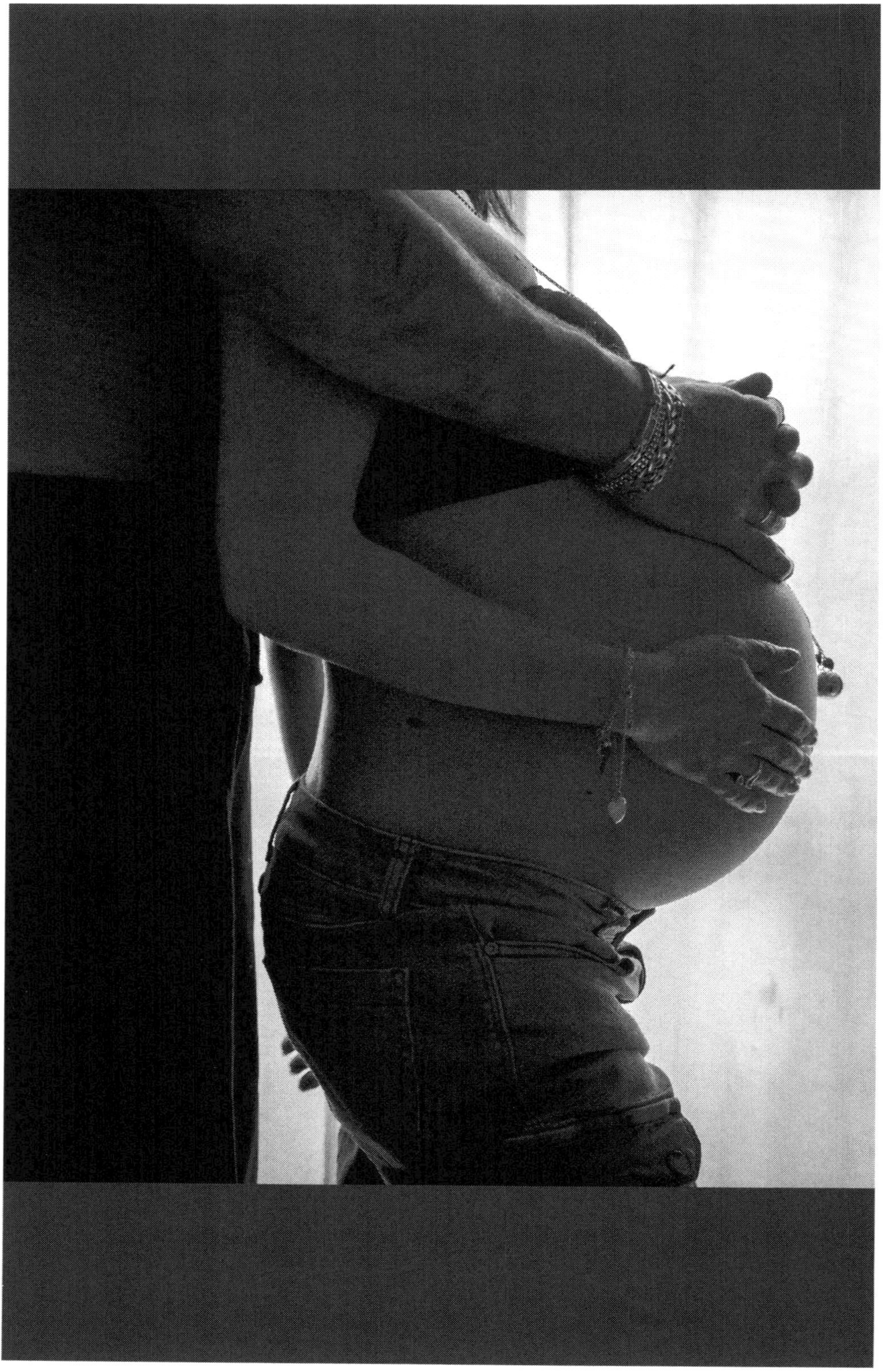

●

She bears the marks of a woman.

She's cried to keep love,

Been stretched to make life,

Been broken by lies,

Been left with heartbreak

And sighs,

But son she's a woman

And she's the kind

You keep by your side

• • •
Broken Footprints Faded Hearts

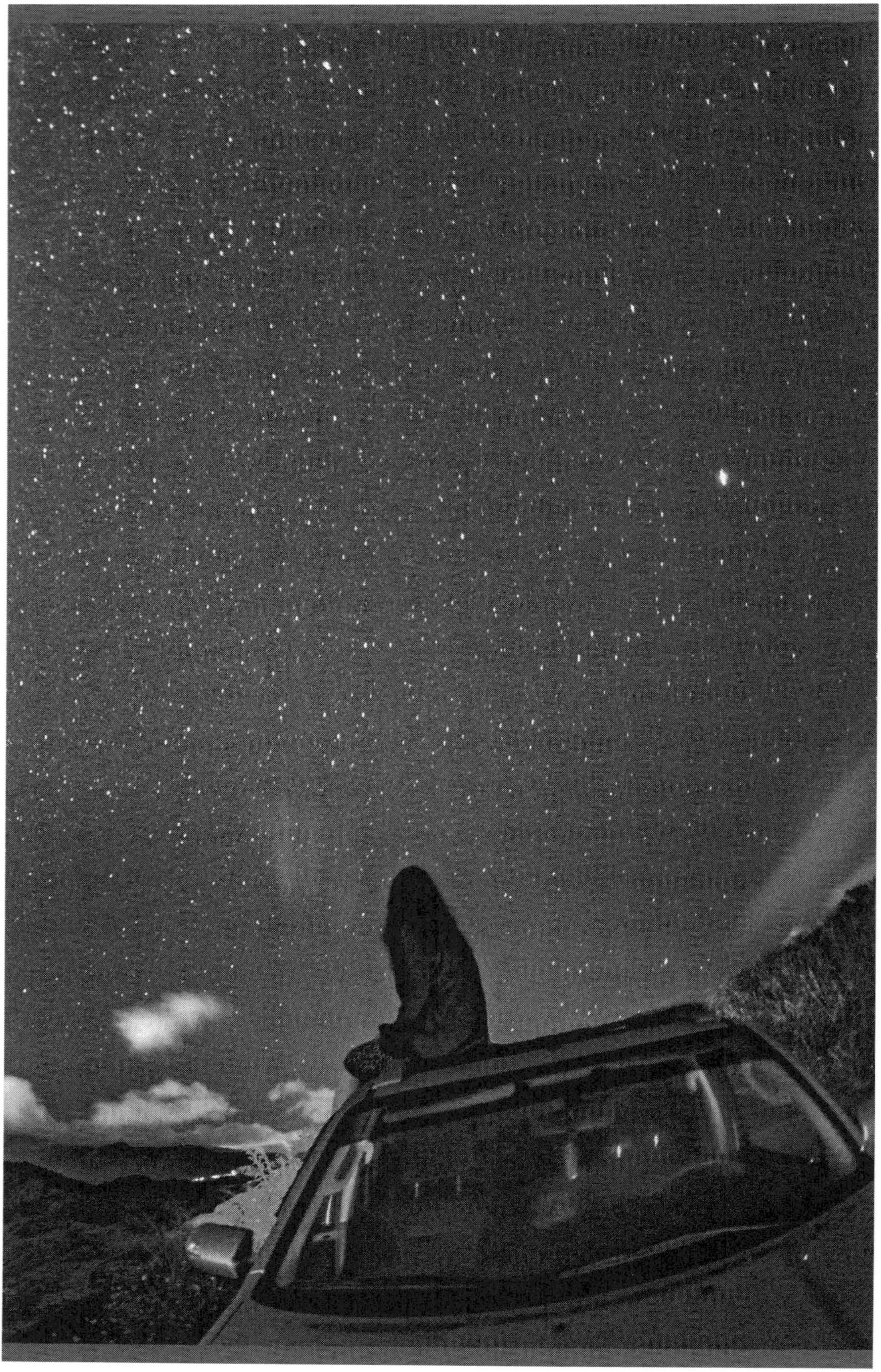

•

She taught me things

Like the sky has stars

A butterfly kiss

Still tickles scars

That the past is good

Cuz it's who we are

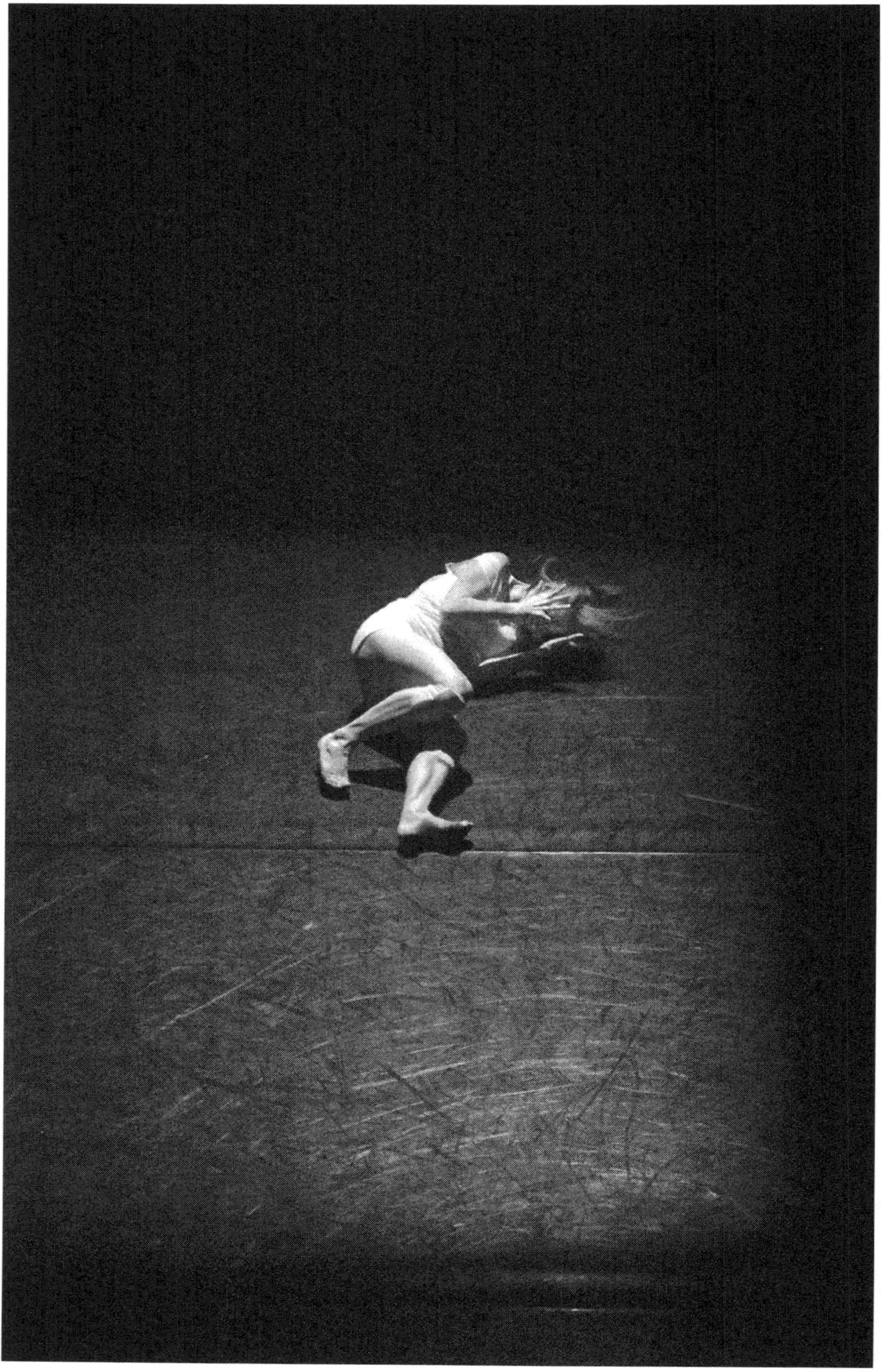

Her very existence

Seemed a peculiar thing

A life-accidental

Marching towards

A purposeful conclusion

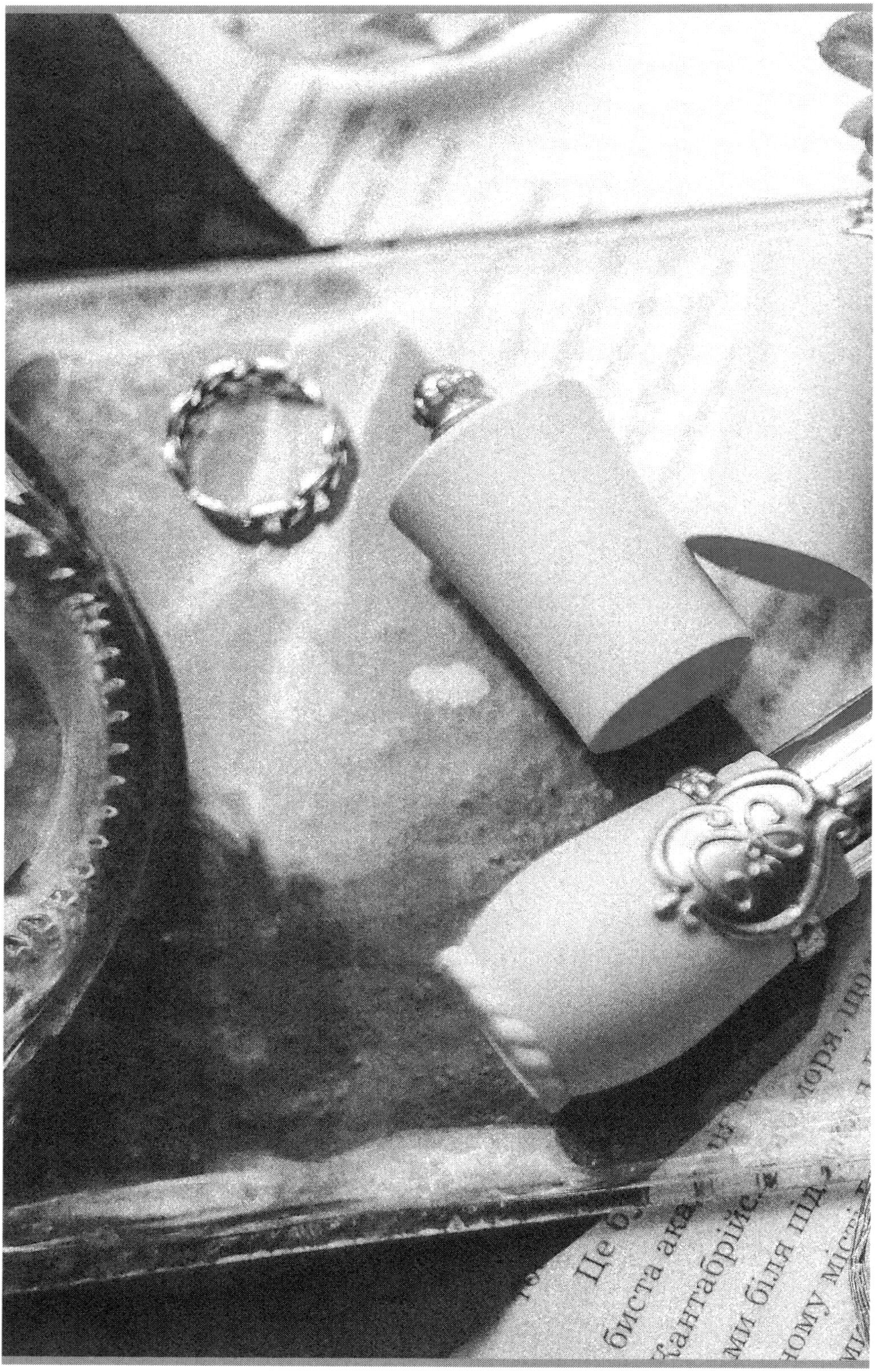

29

●

She hid momma's lipstick
Behind her back
Papa saw it anyway
"Baby, that's a toy for someday.
Cuz your mother knows
She's always prettiest
When it rains.
That right there
Is someone else's idea
Of who you are."
Sixteen and she's using paint
To cover how in-between she seems.
Papa sees.
"Baby, that's okay.
We all need time
To see what your mother already knows
She's always prettiest
When it rains

● ● ●
n.a.denmon

That right there
Only makes a perfect you
Just the same."
Twenty-one.
She's a master
Art to look on
Papa, he's long since gone.
Umbrella hangs hopeless
Over her canvass. I search for words
Her faithless mascara runs away
"Baby, it's okay.
I'm sorry for today
Let this sky wash away the pain.
So you can know
What I already know
You're always prettiest
When it rains"

Broken Footprints Faded Hearts

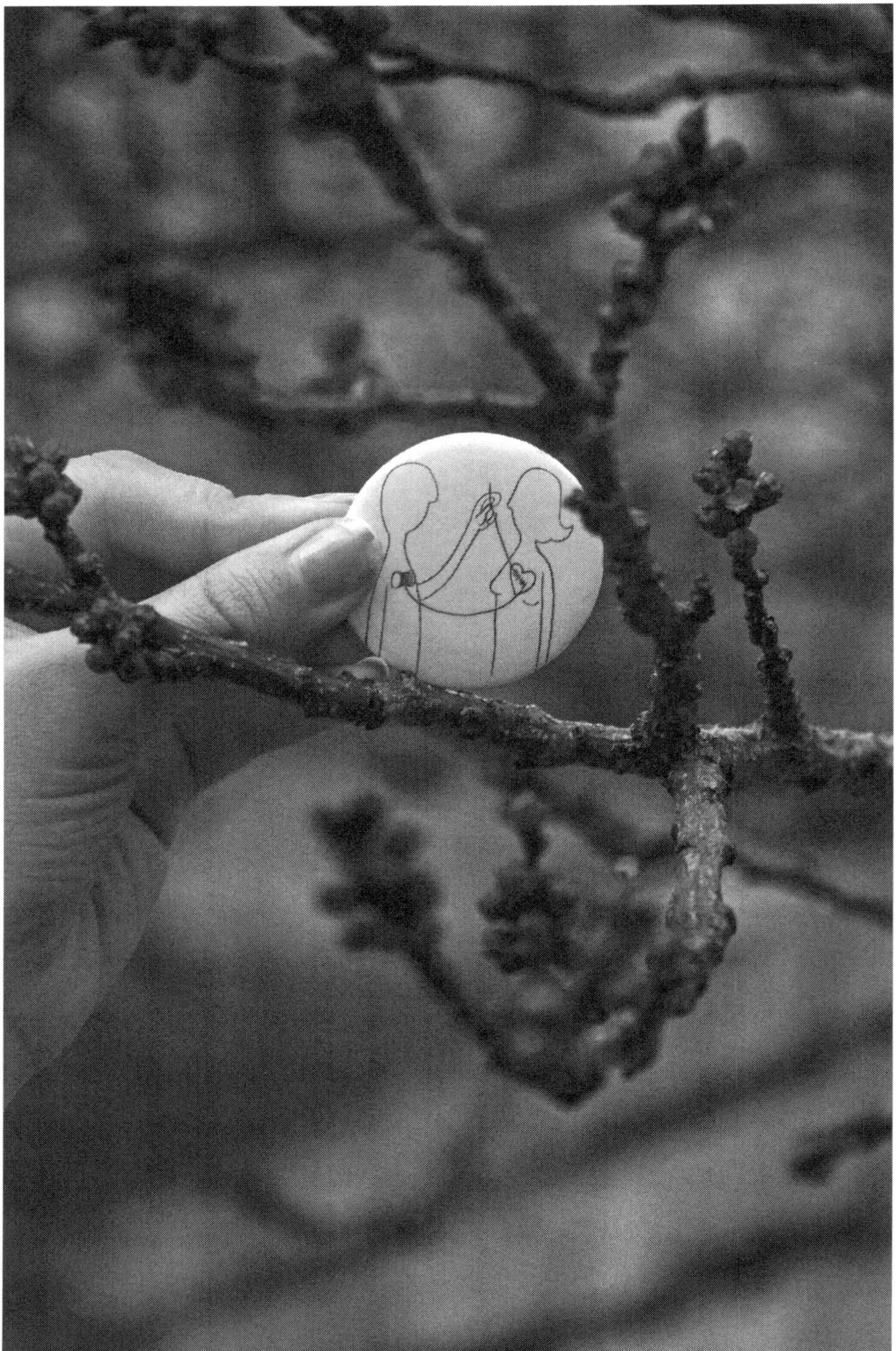

●

In her room of broken hearts

She became Picasso

Fashioning love anew

Nearly the same but different

In every way that mattered

● ● ●
Broken Footprints Faded Hearts

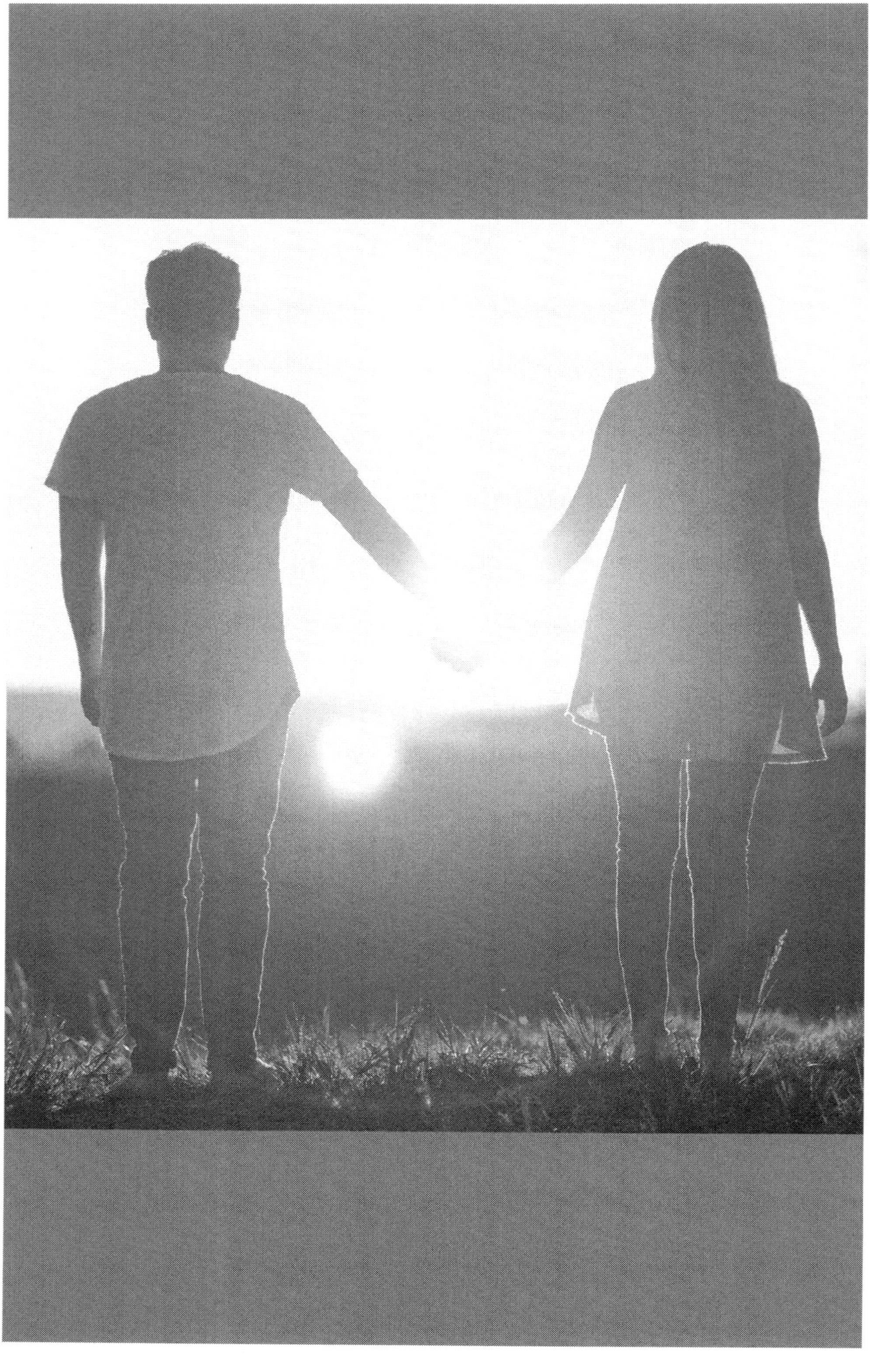

One day you'll find him

And he'll never make sport out of you,

Or pretend that you're a hobby

To be discarded at his whim.

He'll be willing to put in the work

Because loving you will be his job

And that job

Will never feel like work

To him

# ME

ME is an exploration of my own trials and tribulations and how they were influenced by living in a shattered home, growing up with a schizophrenic mother, being take away from my mother at an early age and coming to terms with the strength and insight this unique upbringing has afforded me.

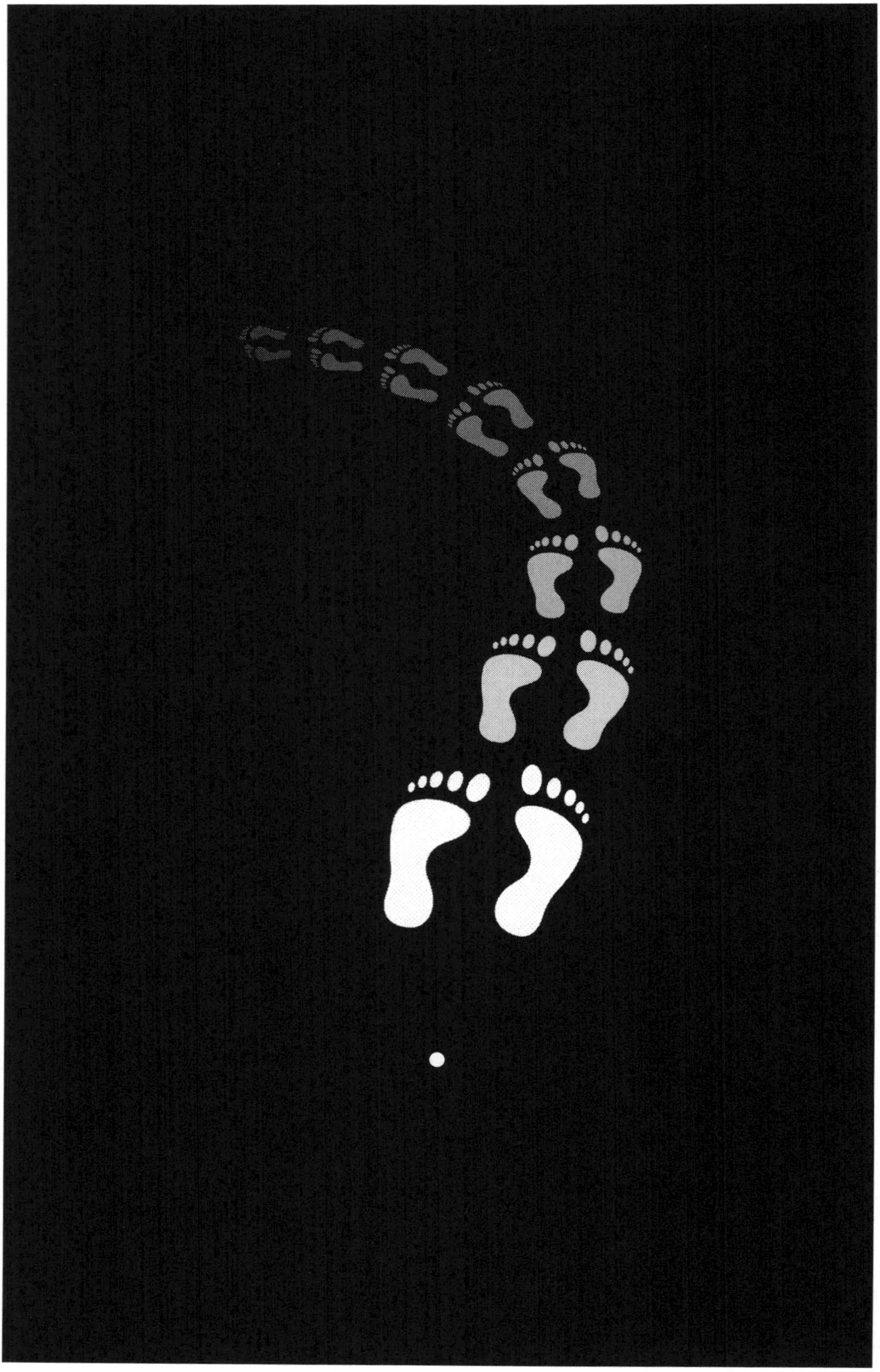

●

I wish you were still around
And that is all
The truth
That I have found

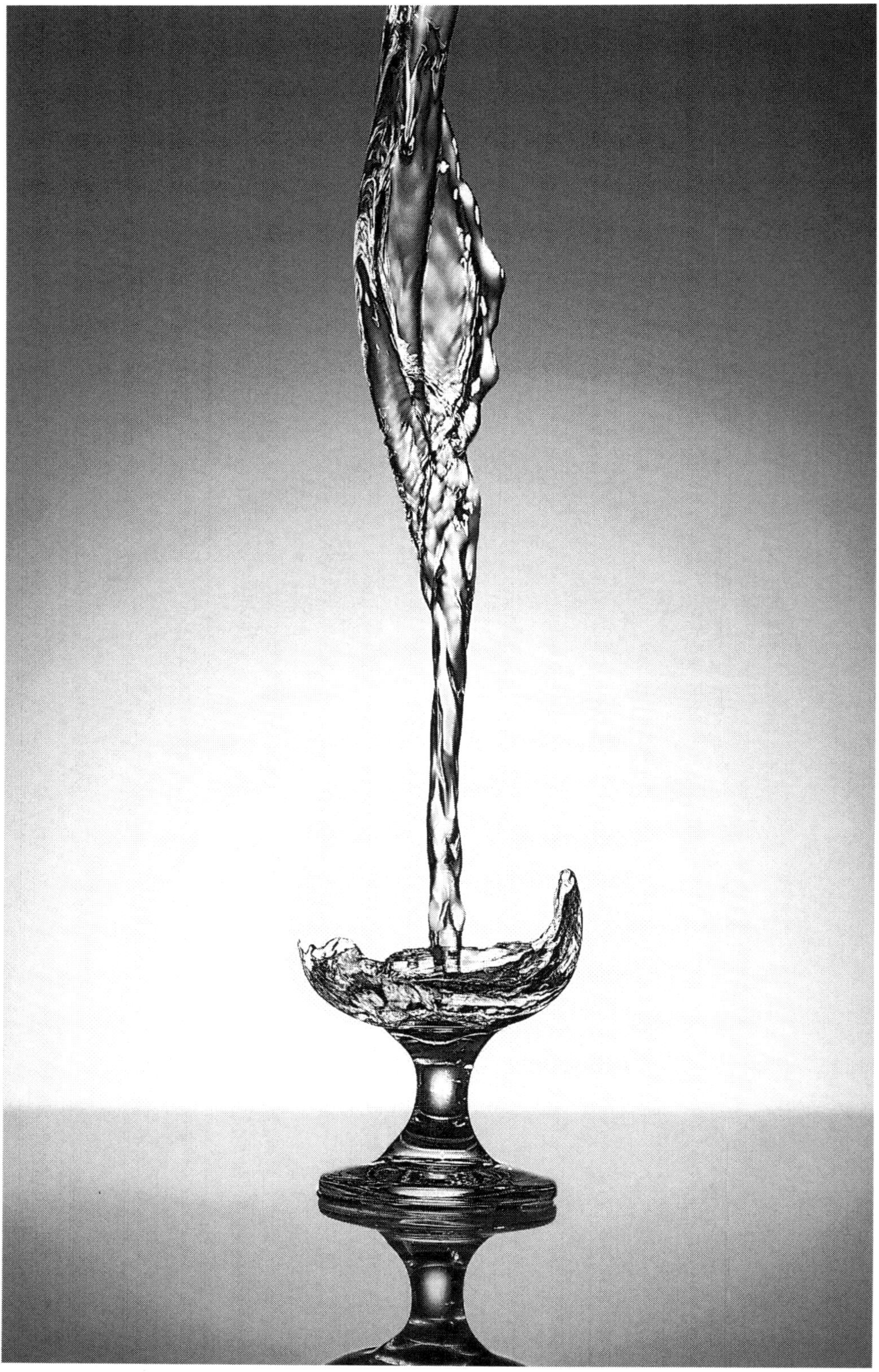

The air hangs heavy with the memory of you

And I cannot see the sun

For the fog of where you were.

A gentle mist wets my cheeks,

With the scent of lilacs,

While my throat still burns

Of self-medicated

Mental anesthetic bourbon

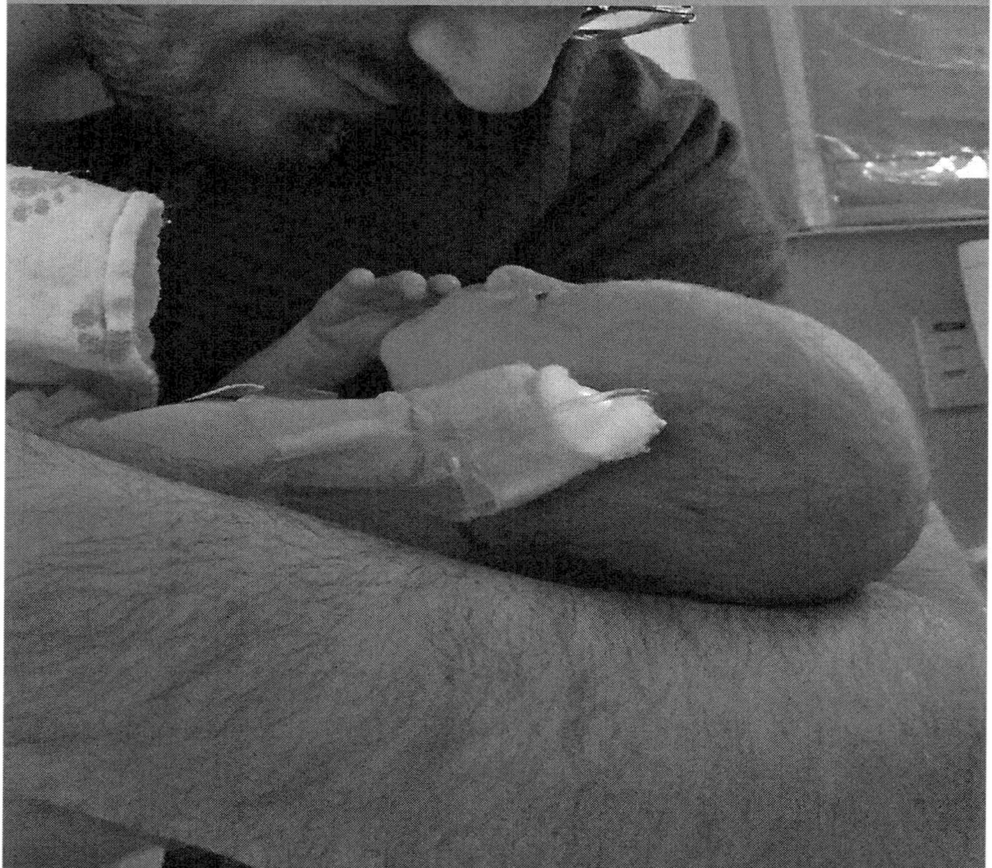

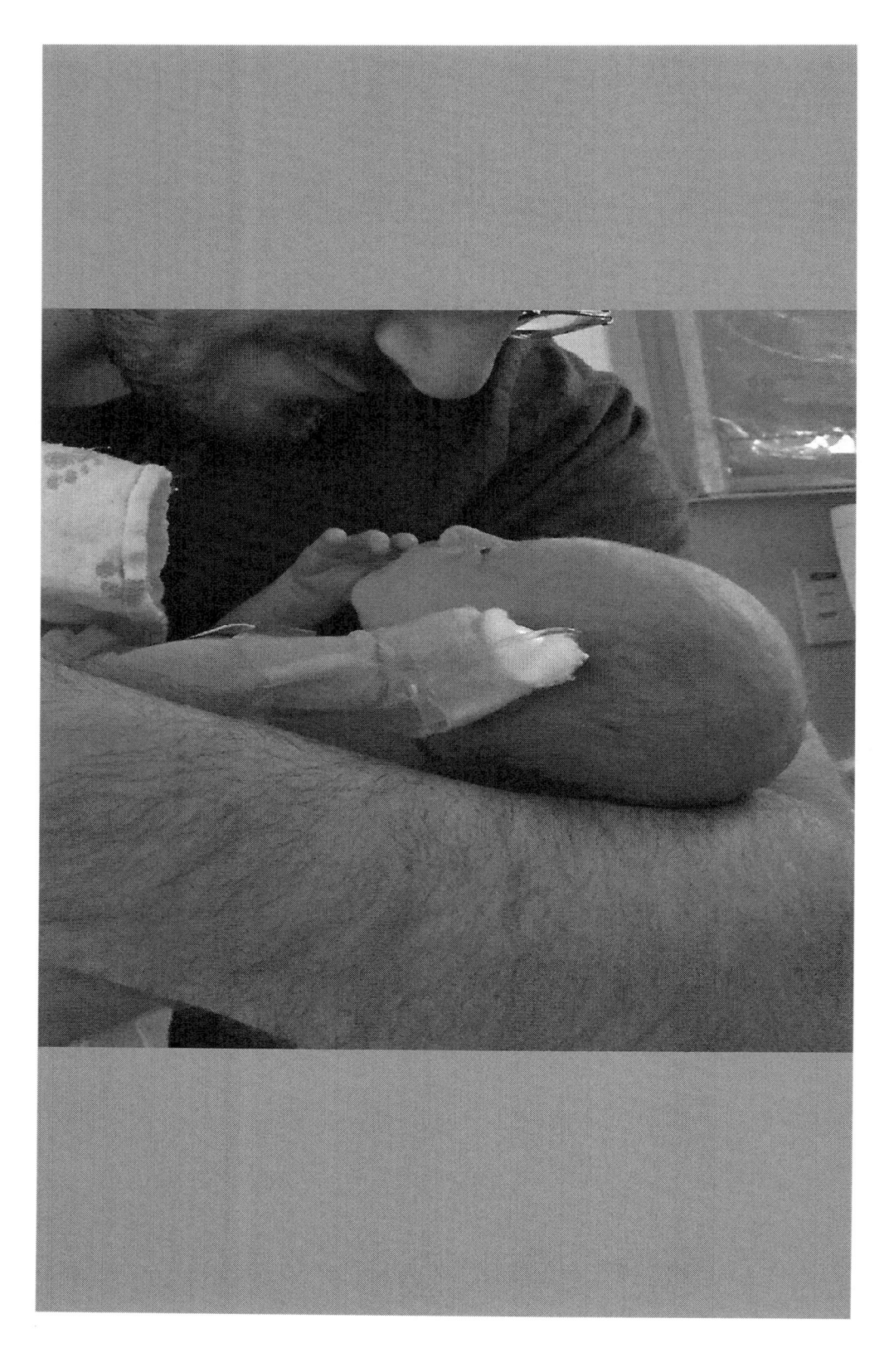

It ain't right to take an infant.

One year is just enough

To give ninety-nine years of hope

Taken away in an instant.

We aren't always given the time we thought we had,

That don't make what we had all that bad.

But it's bitter sweet even though I'd never change

The fact that we'd one day meet. Life sure ain't fair

Cuz if it was, God woulda gave us a bigger share.

But if you gave me the choice, I'd take that moment

For all the hours after. I'd take the memory

And all the pain that drives me insane,

When I'm alone

Remembering the dream and trying to hold it

Before dawn comes again, and life makes me

Go on further from then. Further from that time,

Way back when,

You put your tiny hand in mine

*Broken Footprints Faded Hearts*

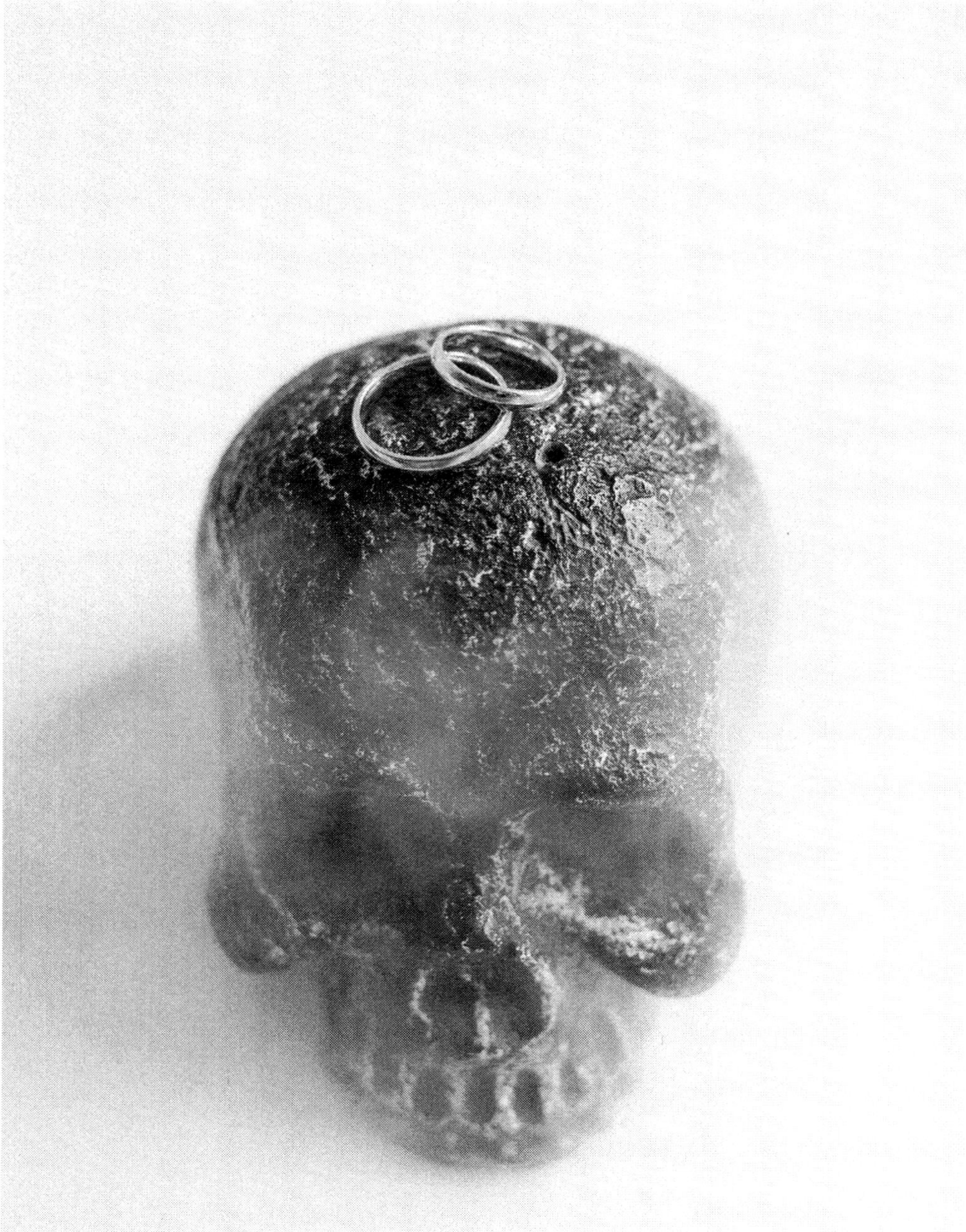

•

She's wrapped around

The bones of me

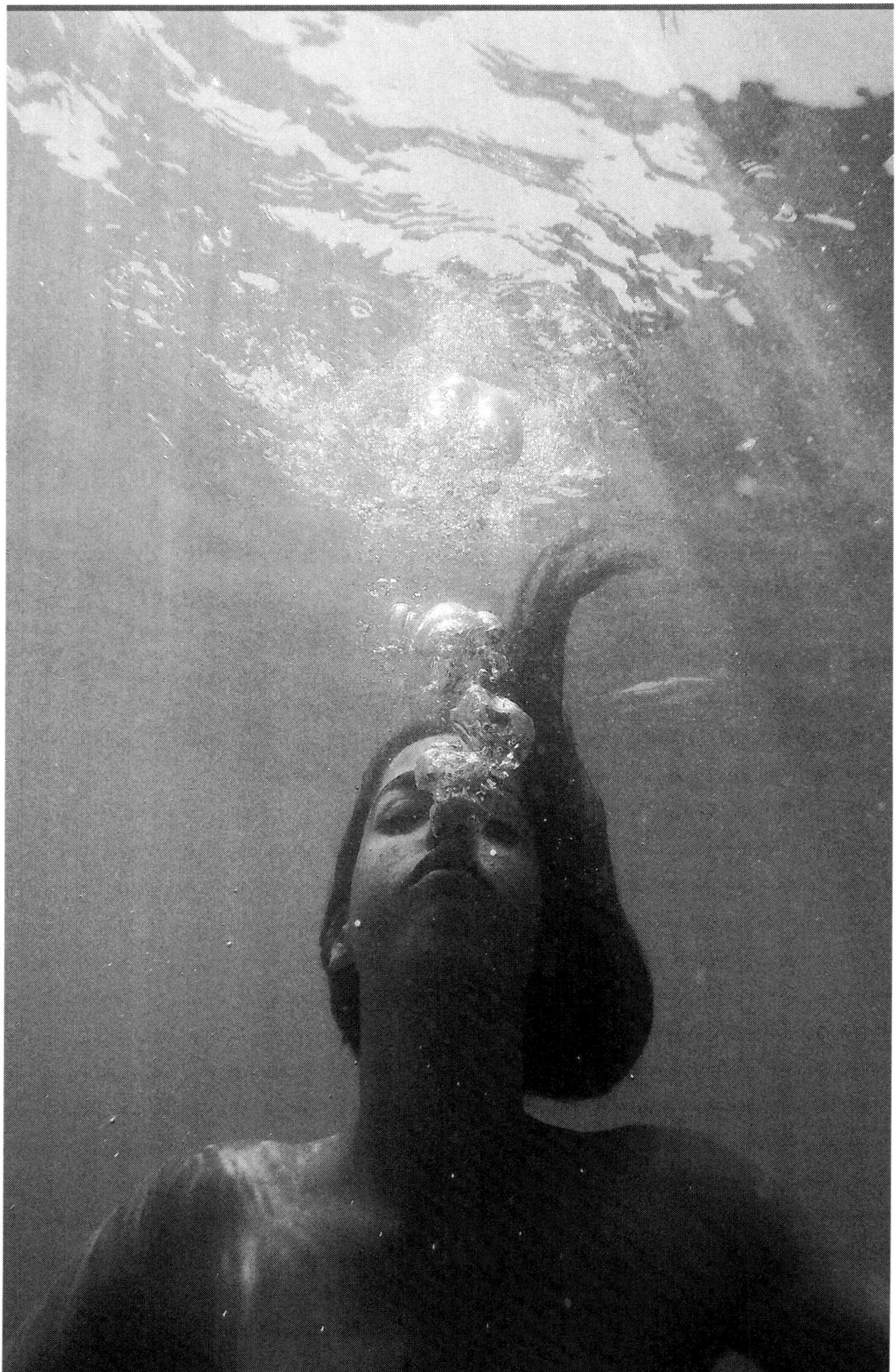

●

She slipped naked

Beneath a moonlit sea

Raining laughter

In sheets of music

At a star struck me

• • •
Broken Footprints Faded Hearts

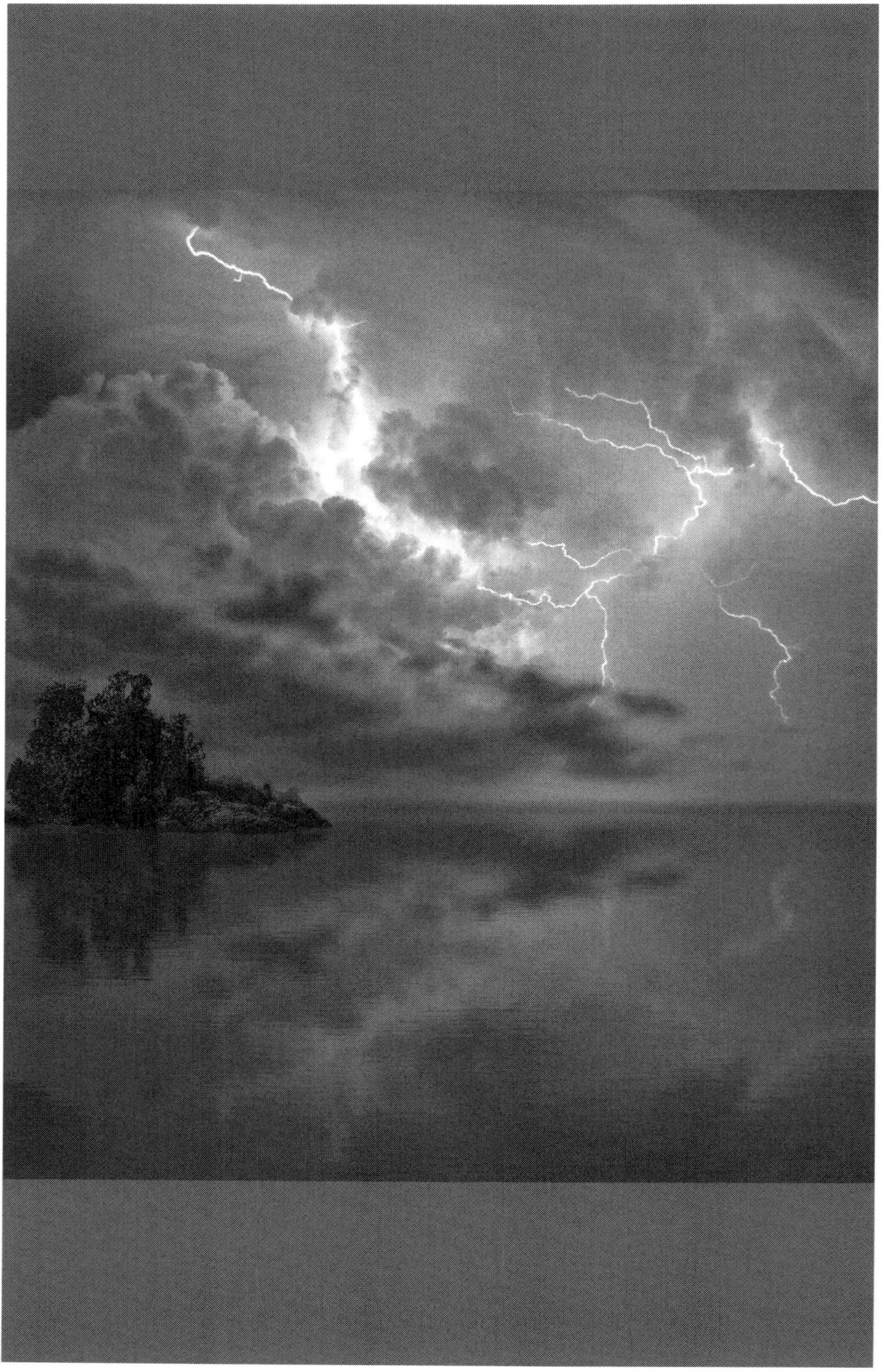

●

Her world was bright and joyful

And drunkenly seductive

And I was an addict for

Anything

That broke my grey

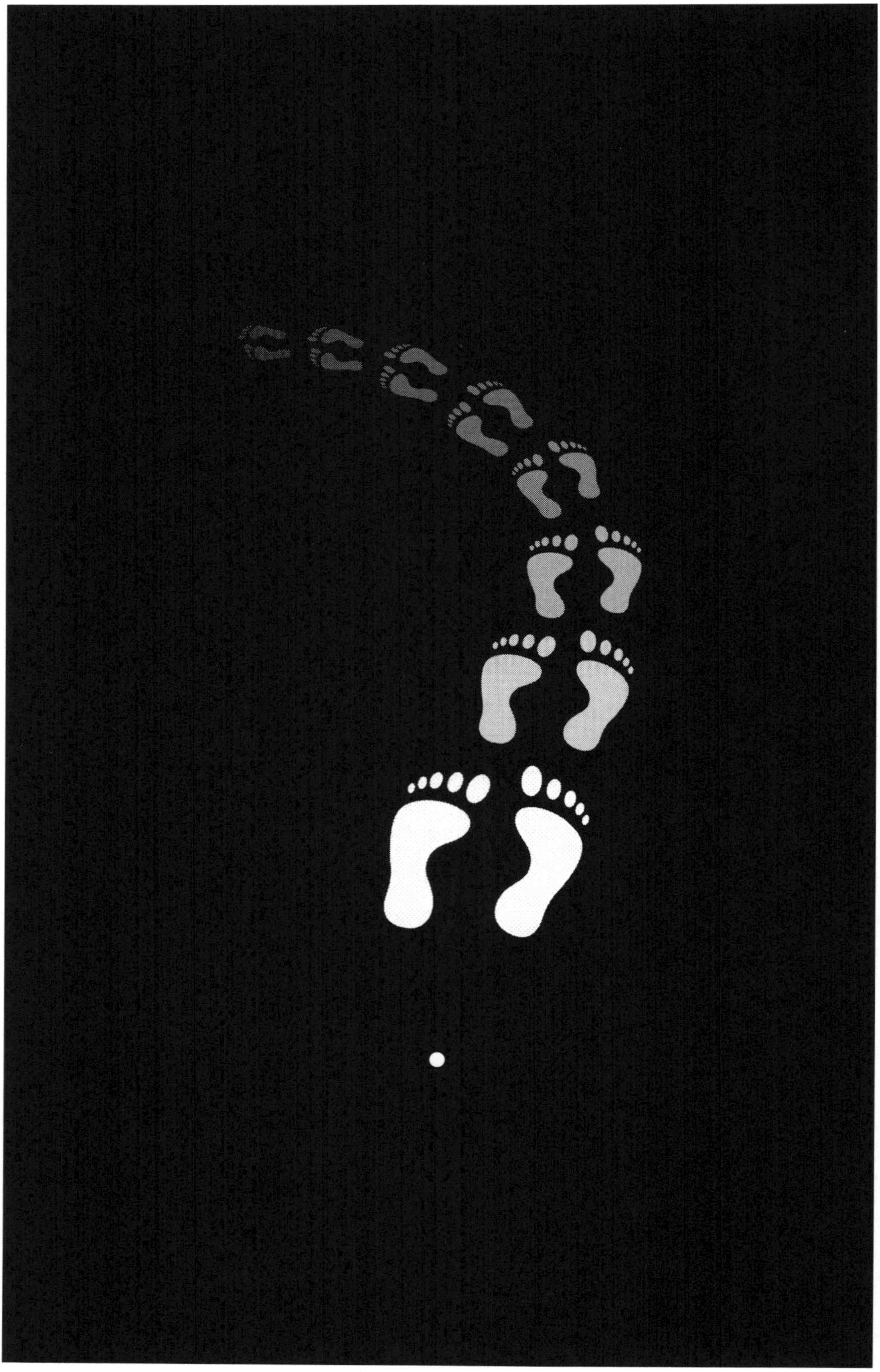

The monster in me
Fears the light
That you give

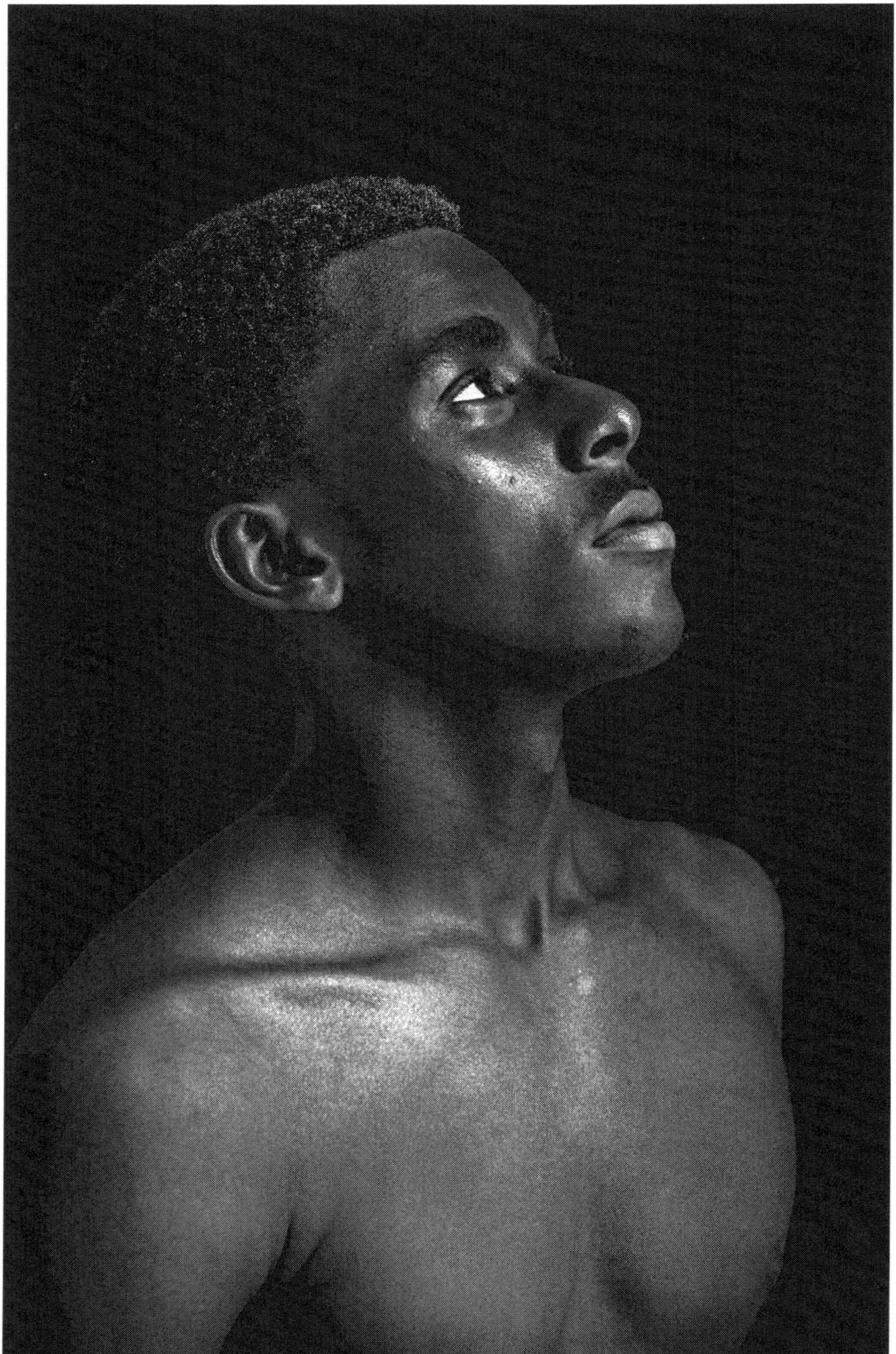

●

I'm in the dark

And I put myself here

A soul tires

Of manufactured light

And the noise

Of neon lies

● ● ●
Broken Footprints Faded Hearts

Rain beats on the window glass,
Giving rhythm to my pain. It's a
Dance I've done a thousand times,
But the memory of you remains
The same.
The midnight hour mourns in harmony
With distant chimes and the darkness
Lends its tears. An emphatic shower
Weeps your name
In gentle rivers
Down my window frame

●

3:30 am and I can still

Remember when

You were my person

Instead of a mental chaser

For cheap house bourbon

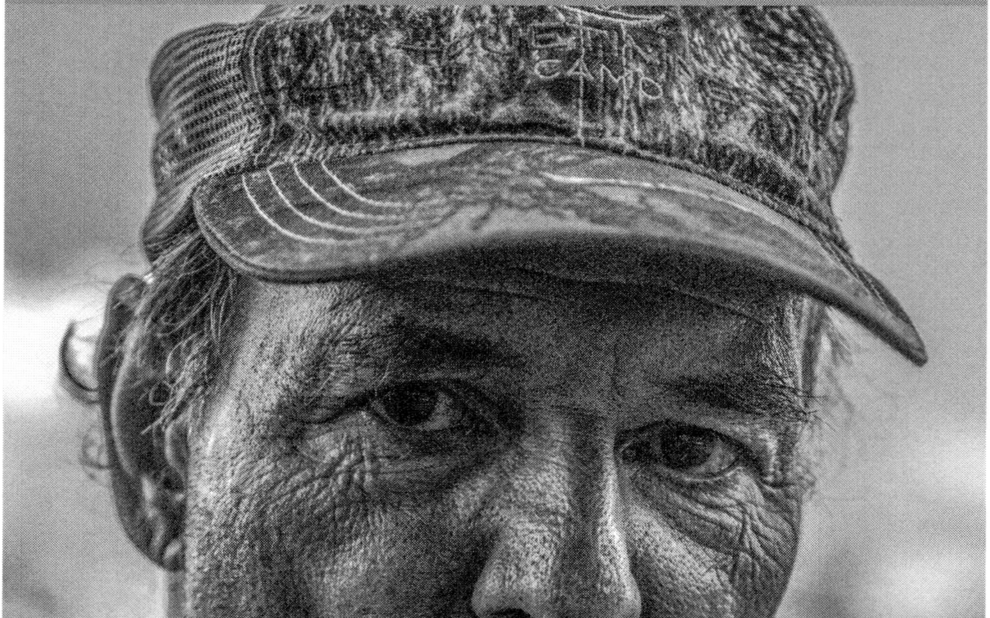
CAMP

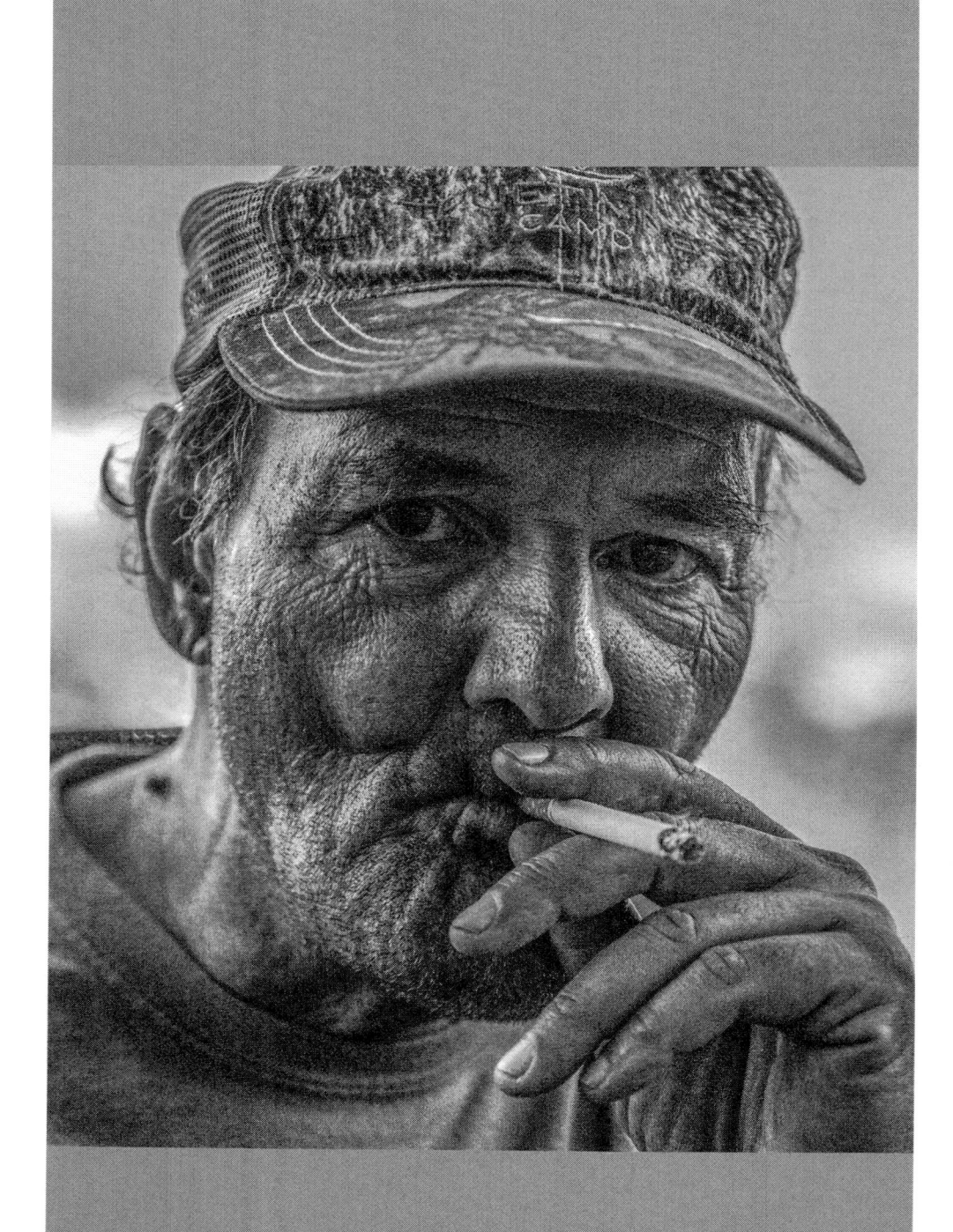

Here I am. Naked.

A little bit fat.

A little bit old.

Got some scars,

So many freckles,

A little less hair

And wrinkles

To tally my cares.

But baby this is what happens

When life ain't fair

When you never fake it,

And take a beating

Through the greatest love story

Ever told.

Don't need to ask me again.

I'd pay that price.

I'm already sold and I'd do it twice.

Cuz life with you

Is always worth repeating

Broken Footprints Faded Hearts

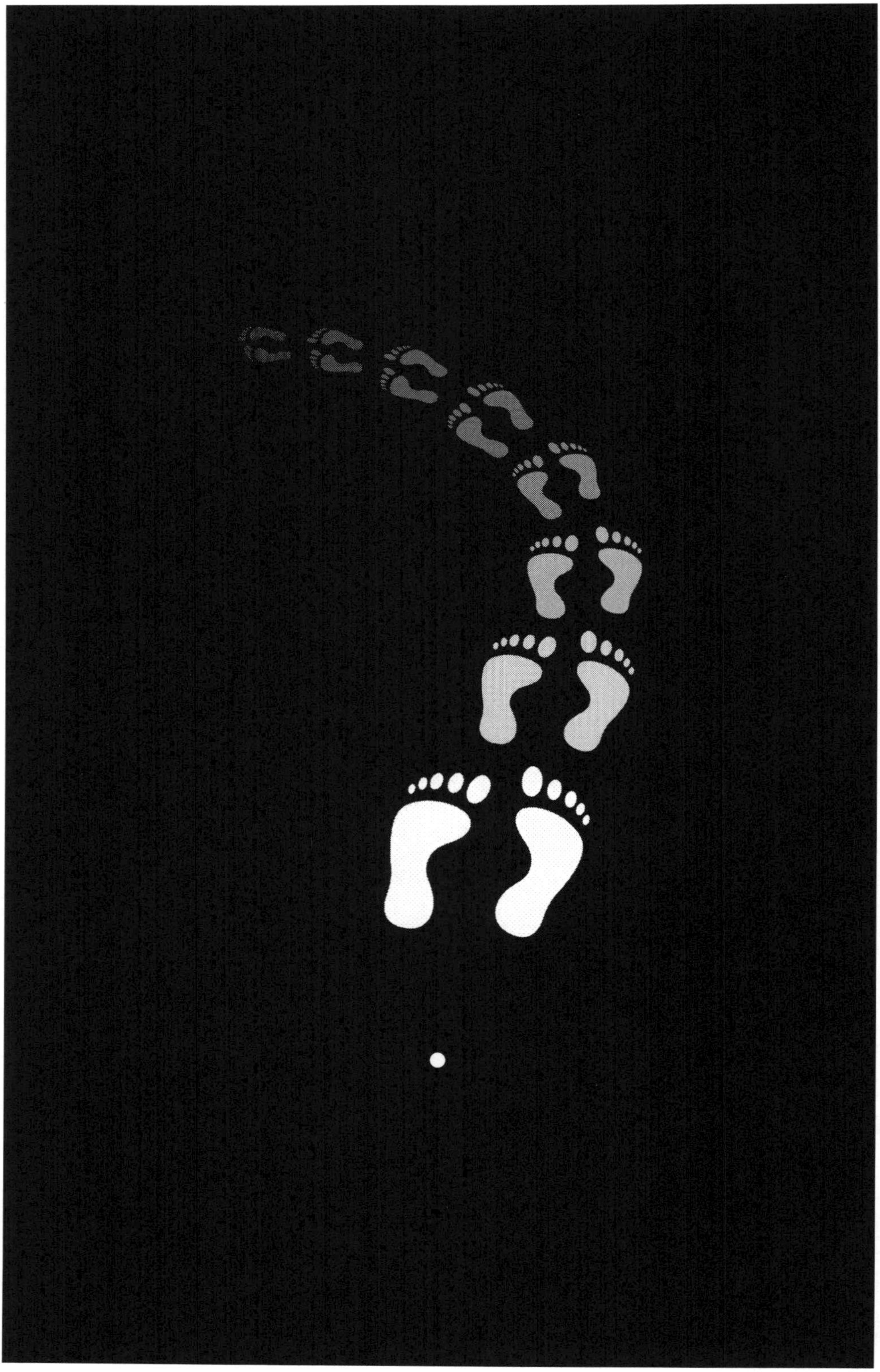

The air holds a chill tonight and
                the drive at 3 am's a losing fight

But not cuz of weighted lids.
                It's a heavy heart that's got me down

And keeps me up more'n the hours ever did.

God I wish you were still around.

Streetlights pass me by like ghosts at eighty

Like the dreams I had that I thought'd never die.

Yeah, there were times I thought I did my most,

But at most I didn't do it right.
                I put the windows down,

Let the wind in as my hopes fly out.

Oh, the air, it's damn chilly tonight. The radio's on

And hears me just right. Wish I could jump

Or turn around but the thing
                just keeps driving itself.

I'd scream if I could but when you can't breathe

It's hard to make a sound.

God I wish you were still around

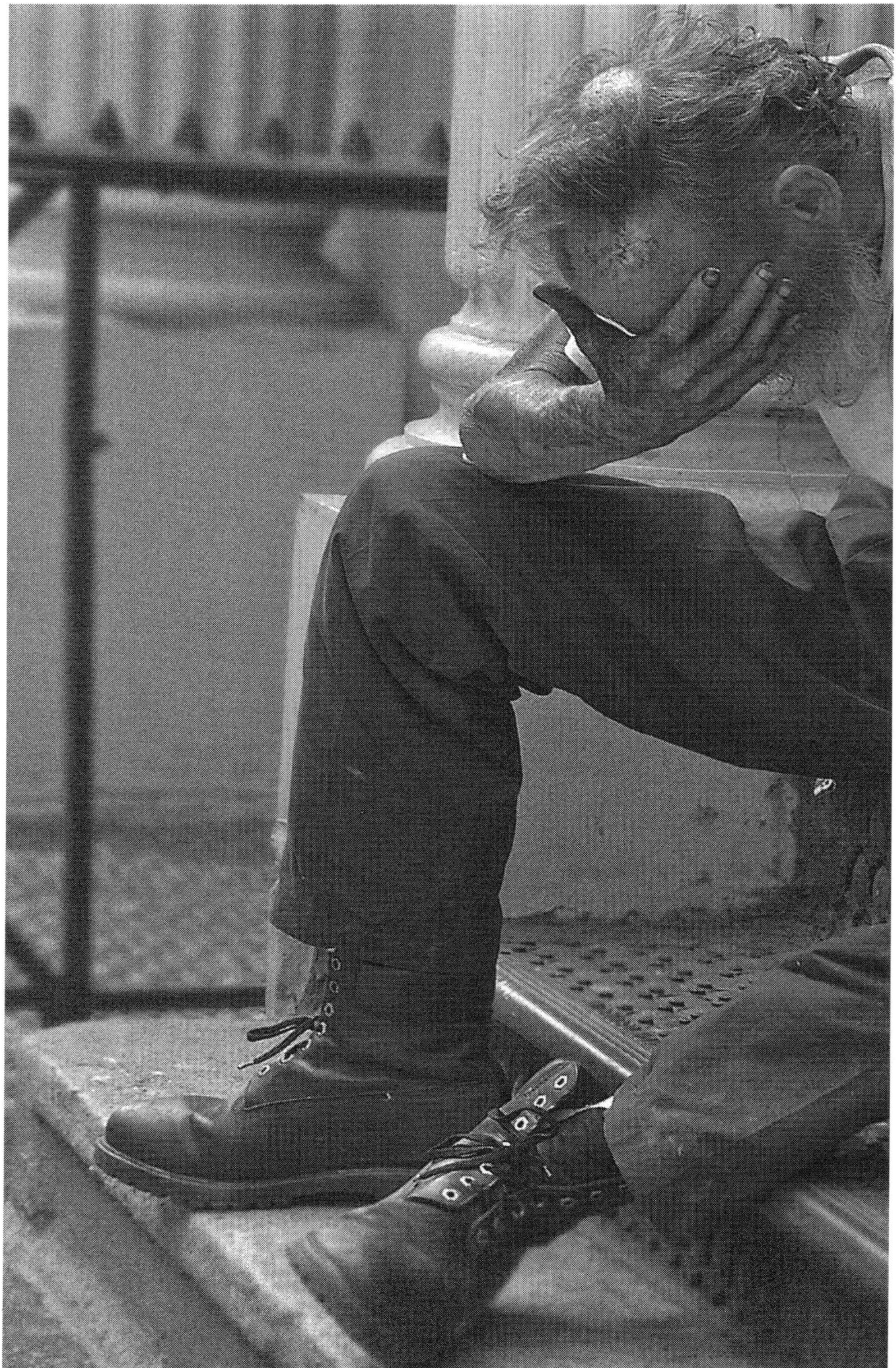

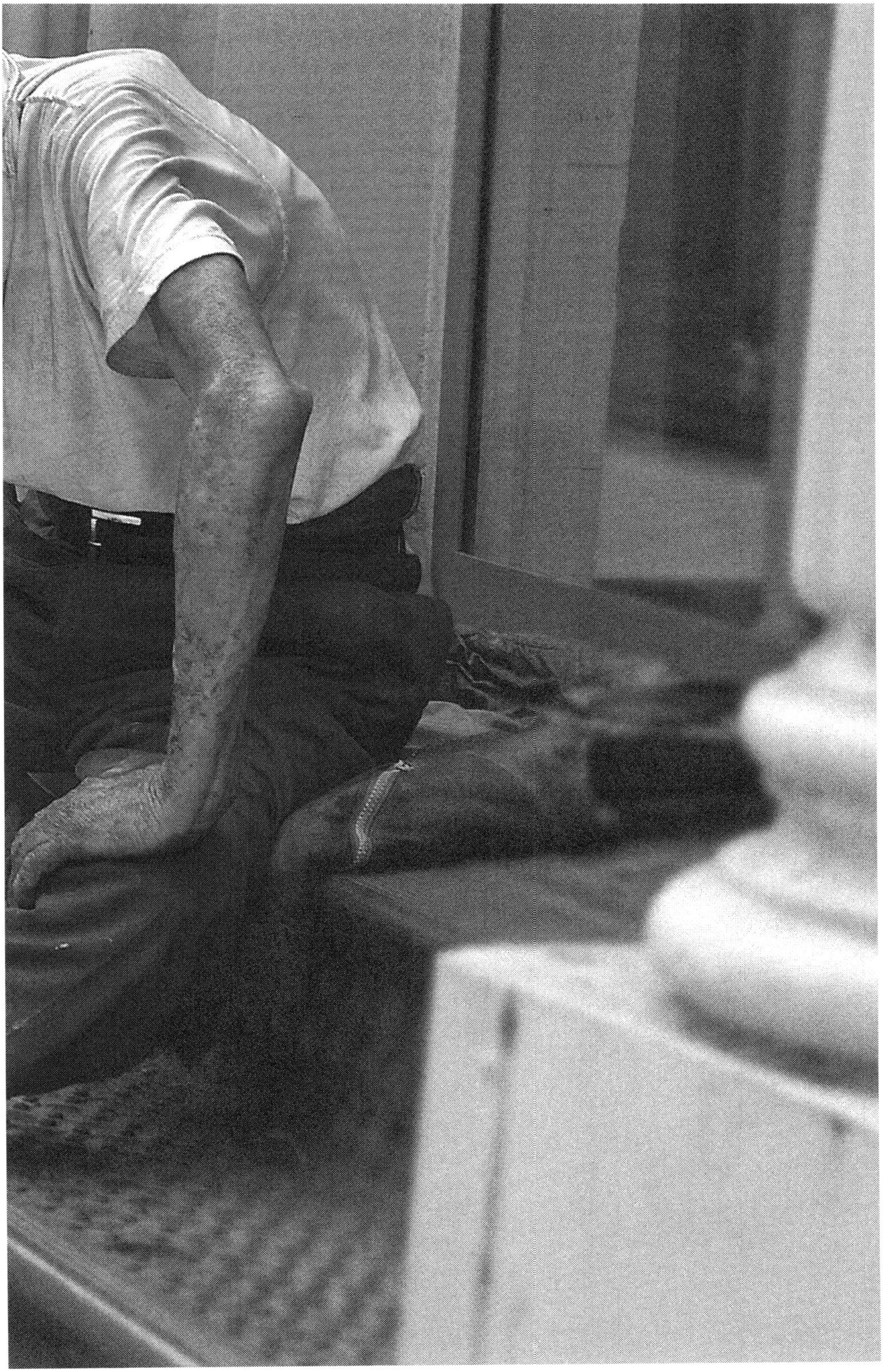

There's a man out on 4th
That shakes cups for quarters.
I watch him from the shop
Sipping coffee in a window
Glass between us.
Everyone he meets
He greets with a smile and a jingle.
So instead of wondering
I just go and ask, "Hey man
How'd you end up out here?"
His name is Frank
Was a father of three
And a doctor too.
Loved his wife and had a life
He loved through and through.
But that was in the days before
The fire that took it all.
So, he shakes a cup for quarters
Cuz he'd rather borrow change
For booze, than remember

n.a.denmon

Times before the sorrow called.
He'd rather sing a jingle
For a jangle and keep the company
Of stars, even if it does get cold
In the winter.
I still think of Frank
That old man on 4th
And wonder if he's cold
Or has he found a place to get warm?
I know, when I left from there,
I was a few quarters poorer
But I heard Frank and his story
And a stranger made me feel
For something real.
And so, hopping on the bus,
I can see in the ways that matter
I left a bit richer
And had a man named Frank
To thank for showing me
One of the many
Faces of us

• • •

Broken Footprints Faded Hearts

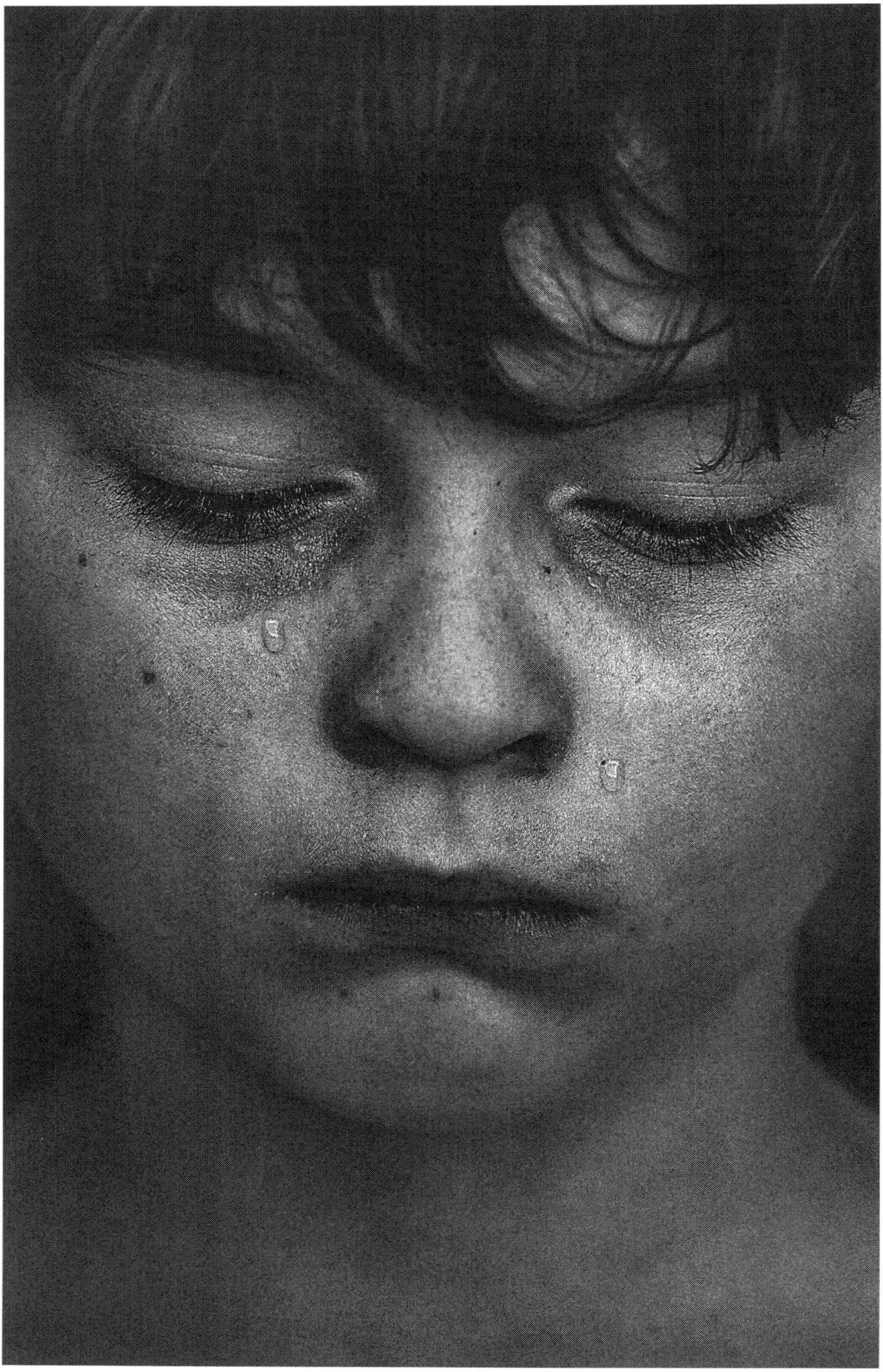

Momma, I love you.

But I think you made me crazy.

Told me the man took my eyes as a baby,

That plastic lives in this head instead.

Said I had a twin, but my brother was born dead.

You were sick, I know.

I don't need a sorry but sometimes I wonder

What did or didn't stick.

Is yellow really yellow or is it red?

Momma, maybe colors were meant to be hazy

Even though it's scary

There's so much beauty in your crazy.

And it took a while, but I love all of you

Always will

Even that bit too

Cuz

It's you

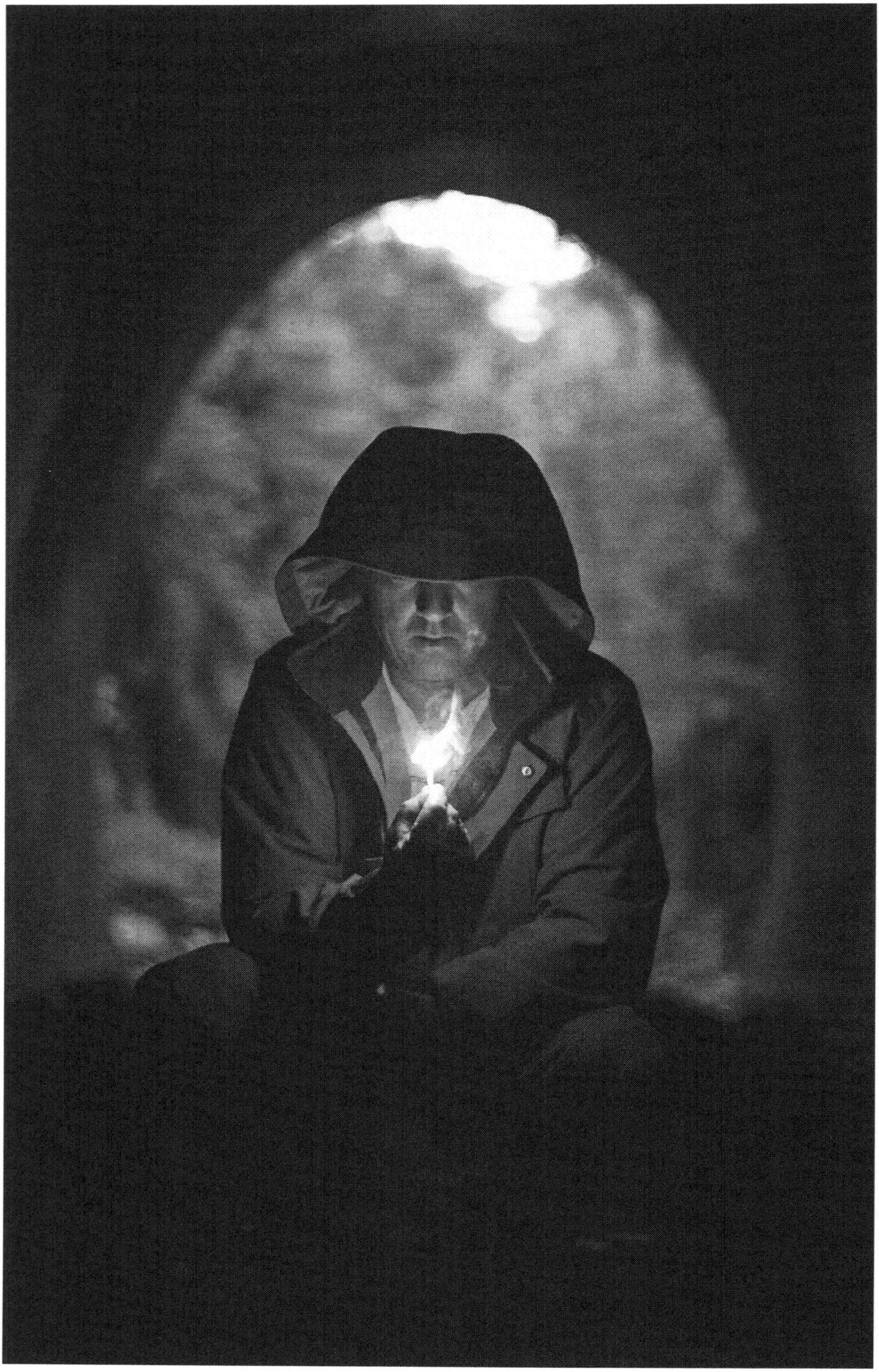

•

Oh Momma, I know this life ain't been easy.

I know you got ghosts this boy of yours won't ever see.

They might take us away, but everything you said, Momma,

That's bound to stay. The thing about a heart of gold,

Is that when life gets dark, it's the thing that's never sold.

Oh, Momma, I know this life ain't been easy.

But you showed me it's the things that shine at night

That help us see

•

Lying in my bed tonight. Can't believe these
Thoughts running in my head. They're keeping
Pace with the ceiling fan. All the things,
I shoulda done instead.
But here I am on a lonely night. Just some
Memories and a sleepless man. Somehow still,
Dreaming of your face, humming all the words
I shoulda said, that play on repeat, inside my head

You're the breath I can't let out.

Hurts like hell to keep you, but

There's no doubt I'll die

Once I let you go.

There goes my life,

Scattered in the wind,

All my love gone

With the world's last bit

Of ironic oxygen

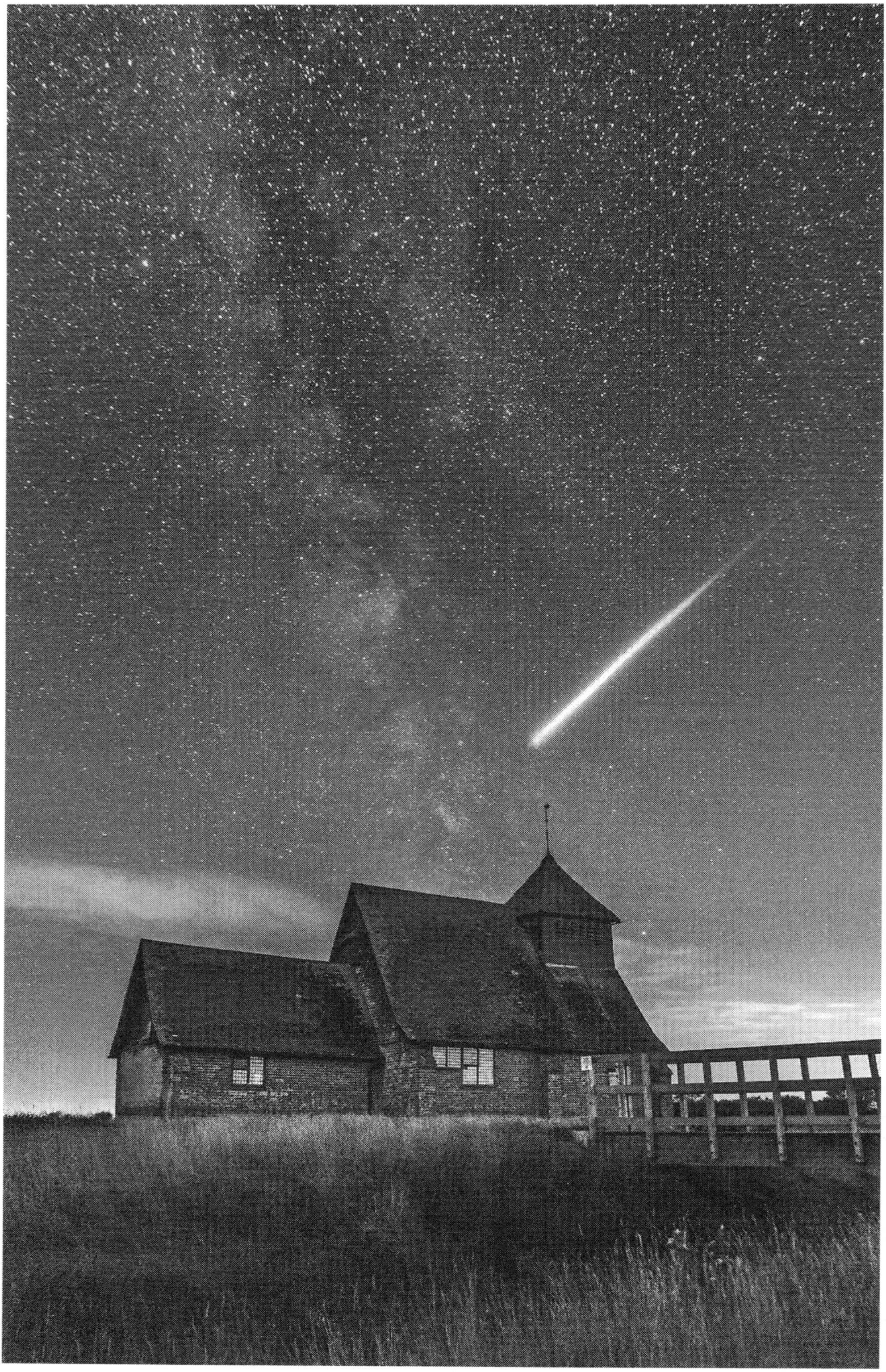

●

On the road, divergent

While lost and all alone

In our mournful last lament

We find paths,

Though overgrown

That lead again,

To home

Broken Footprints Faded Hearts

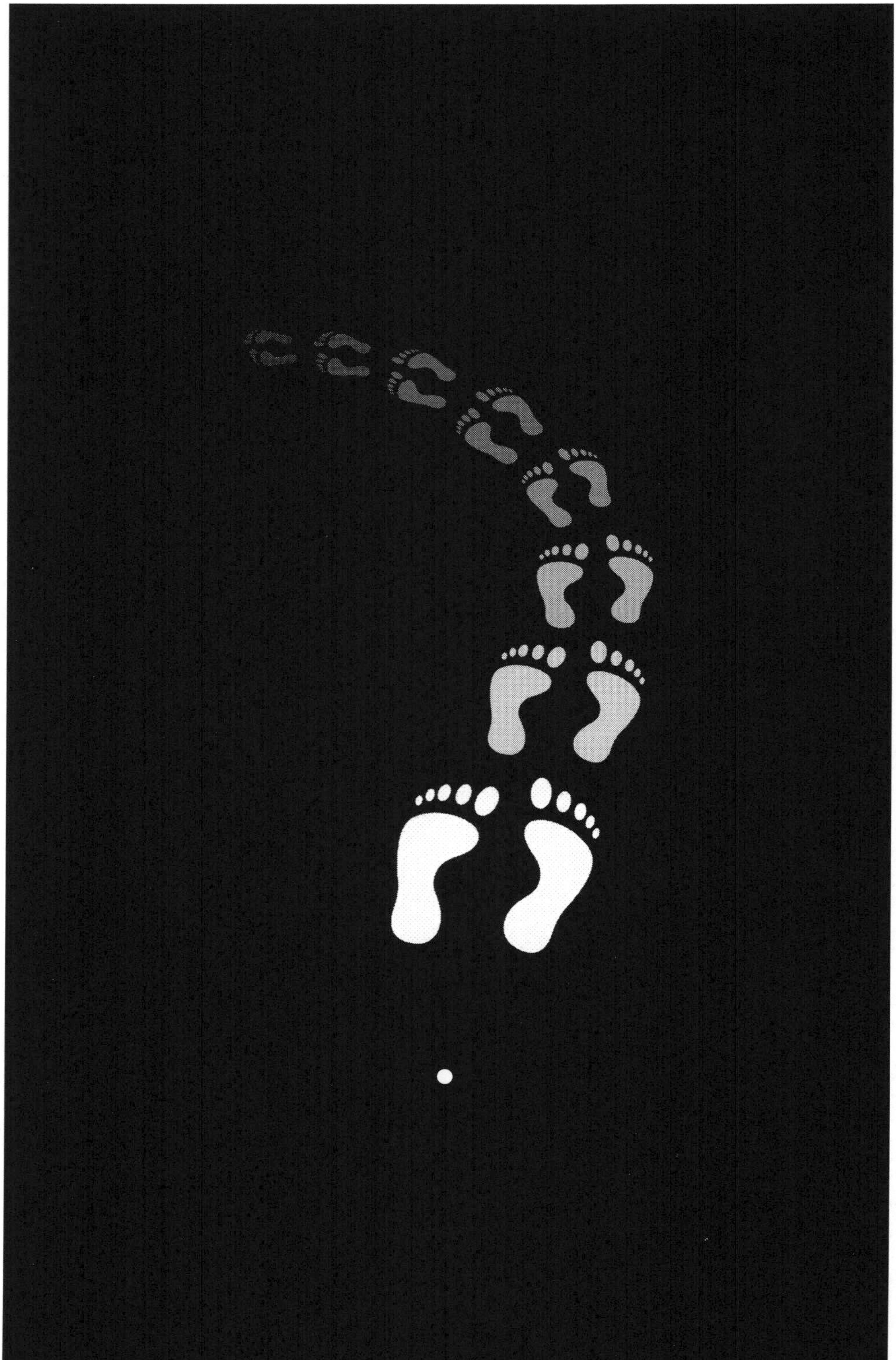

●

Loving her is poison

And still I drink it down

She'll be my

Sadistic hearted suicide

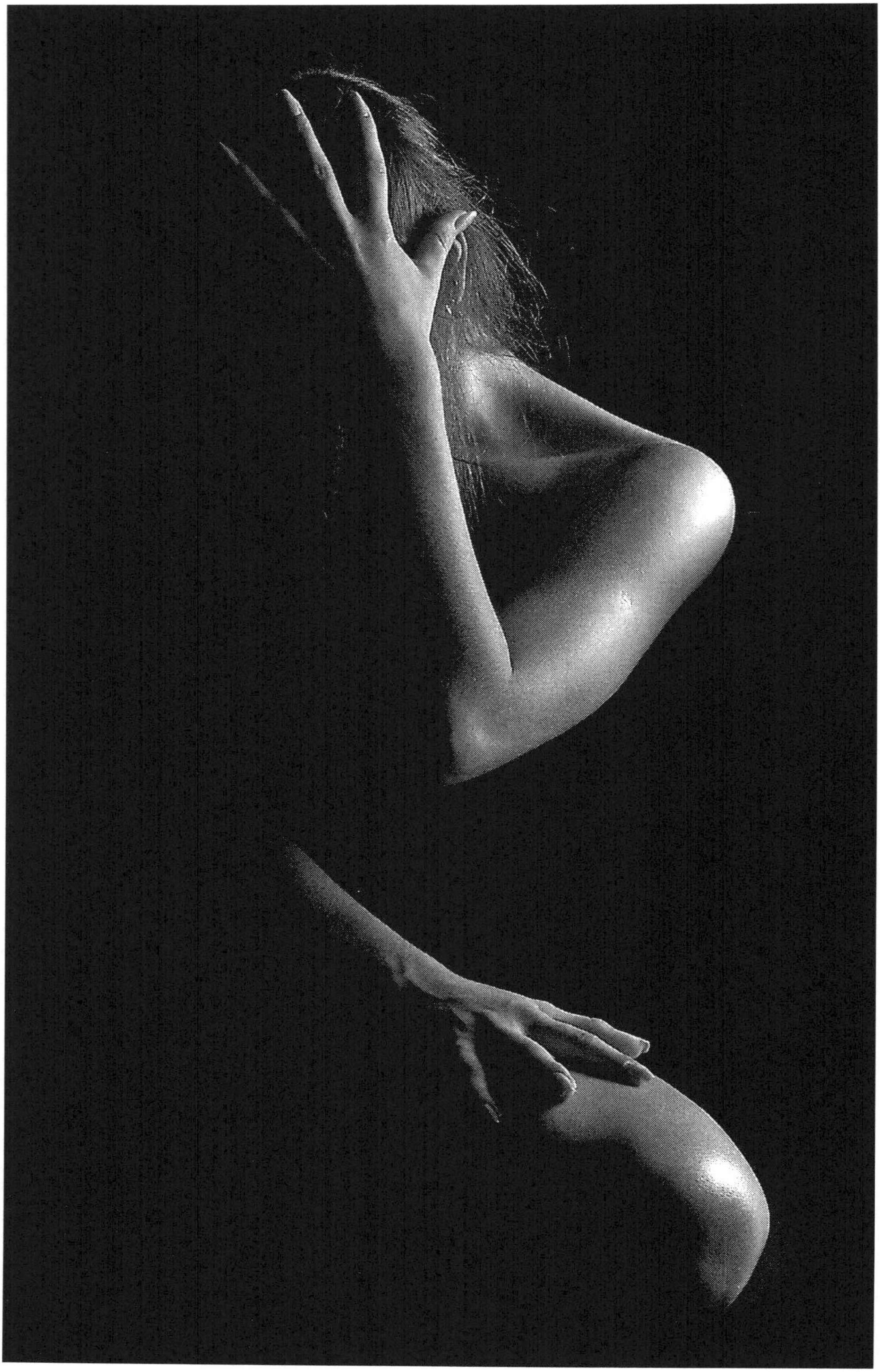

•

You lost your one great love

Because you forgot to love her greatly

She grew her love in the shadow

Of places you did not tread,

For lack of want, or courage.

So new roots took hold

In her heart of darkness

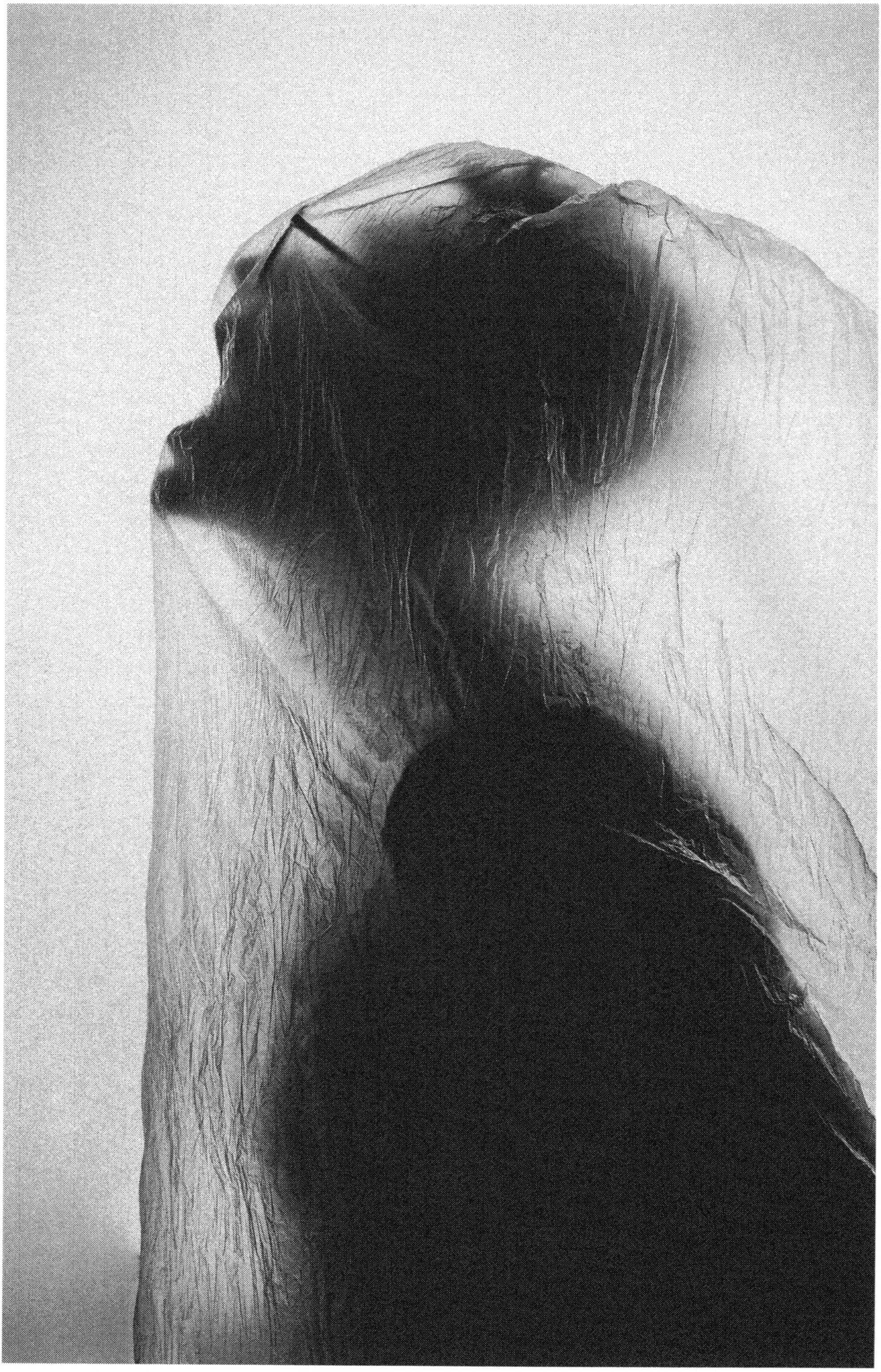

•

What pure torture
To scream so loud
And not be heard

Beware
Those that would
Know your truth
So that they might
Tailor their lies

●

To have lost
Is to have had
For the having
I am thankful

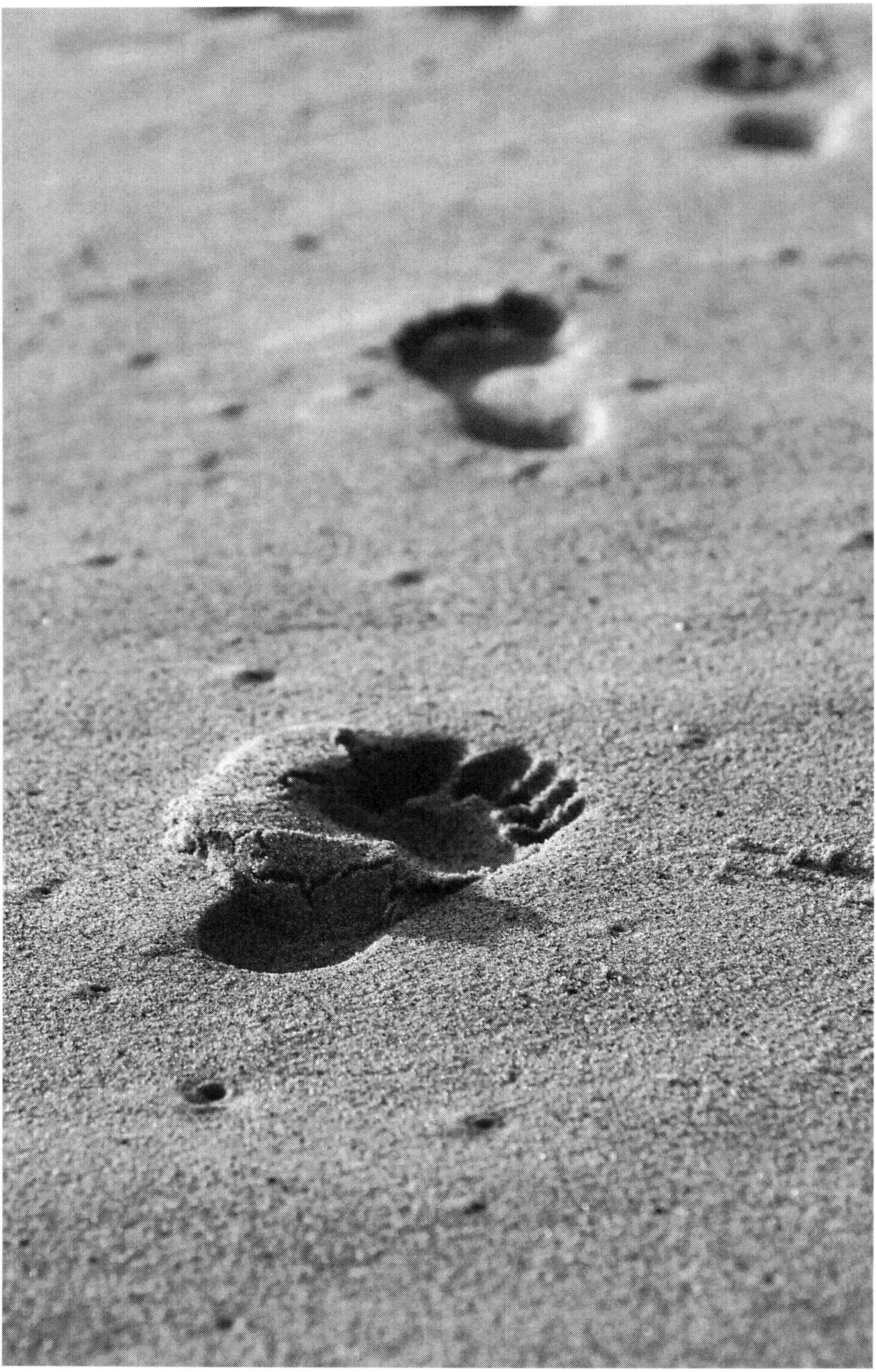

●

Love hard. Live well.

And be okay leaving

Footprints

That wash away

• • •

Broken Footprints Faded Hearts

# THEM

THEM is a brief focus on the forces around us and how they appear at times to pull humans apart from one another. The creation of rules and artificial boxes and categories create these imaginary constructs that can largely be unnecessary at best and suffocating of the individual spirit at worst.

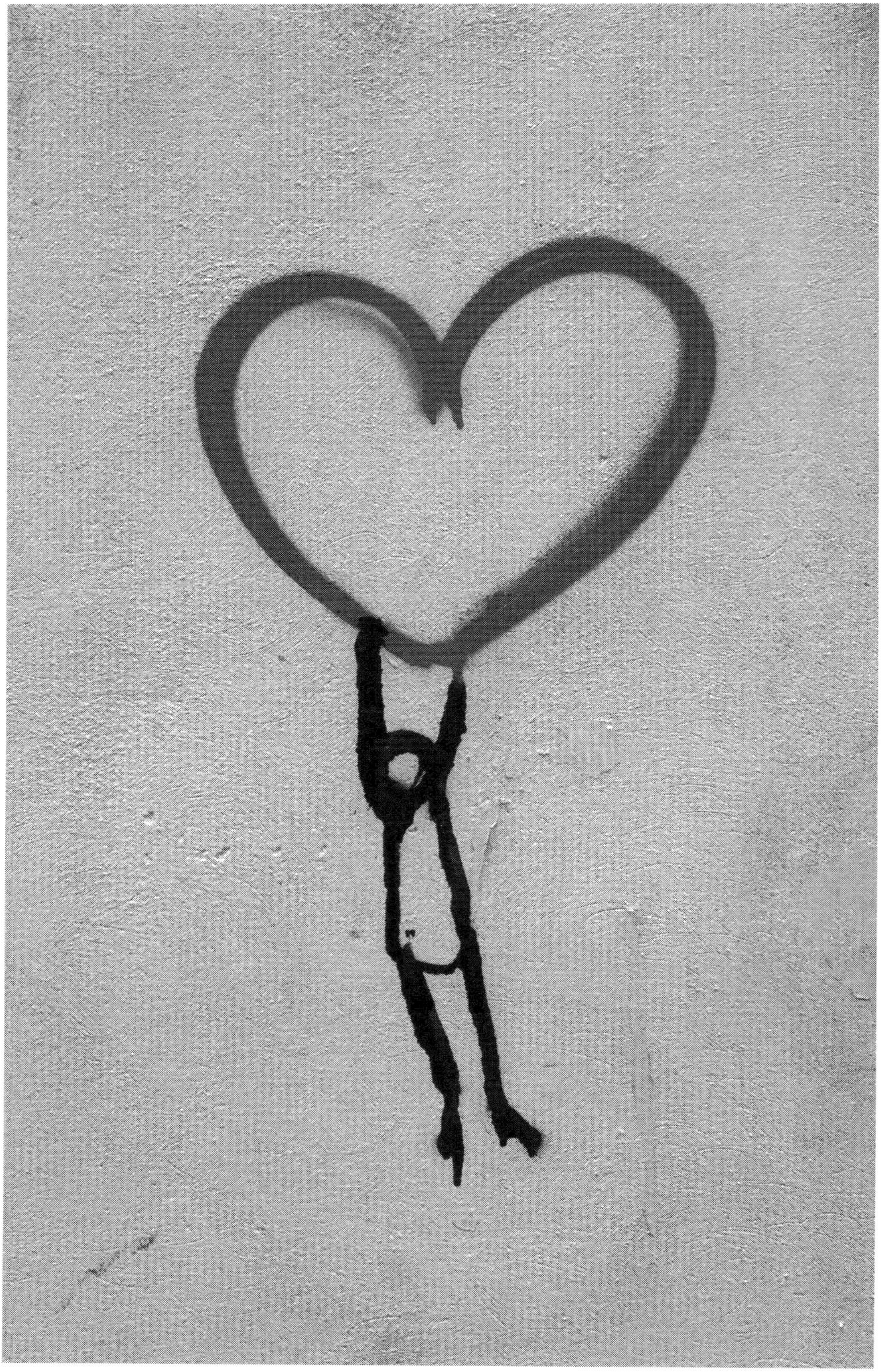

•

Let's talk about love, cynics. It's easy to pretend like we don't feel the truth of moments. It's even easier to throw shade at people that allow themselves these occasions of pure humanness. What you gotta ask yourself there, champ, is why don't you?

I get it.

We all get hurt sometimes and sometimes it's nice to peer into the darkness. But don't get caught staring into that onyx reflection. It's distorted. It's a funhouse mirror of what's right behind you. There is a world of love out there, give it a shot. Isn't it about time?

• • •
Broken Footprints Faded Hearts

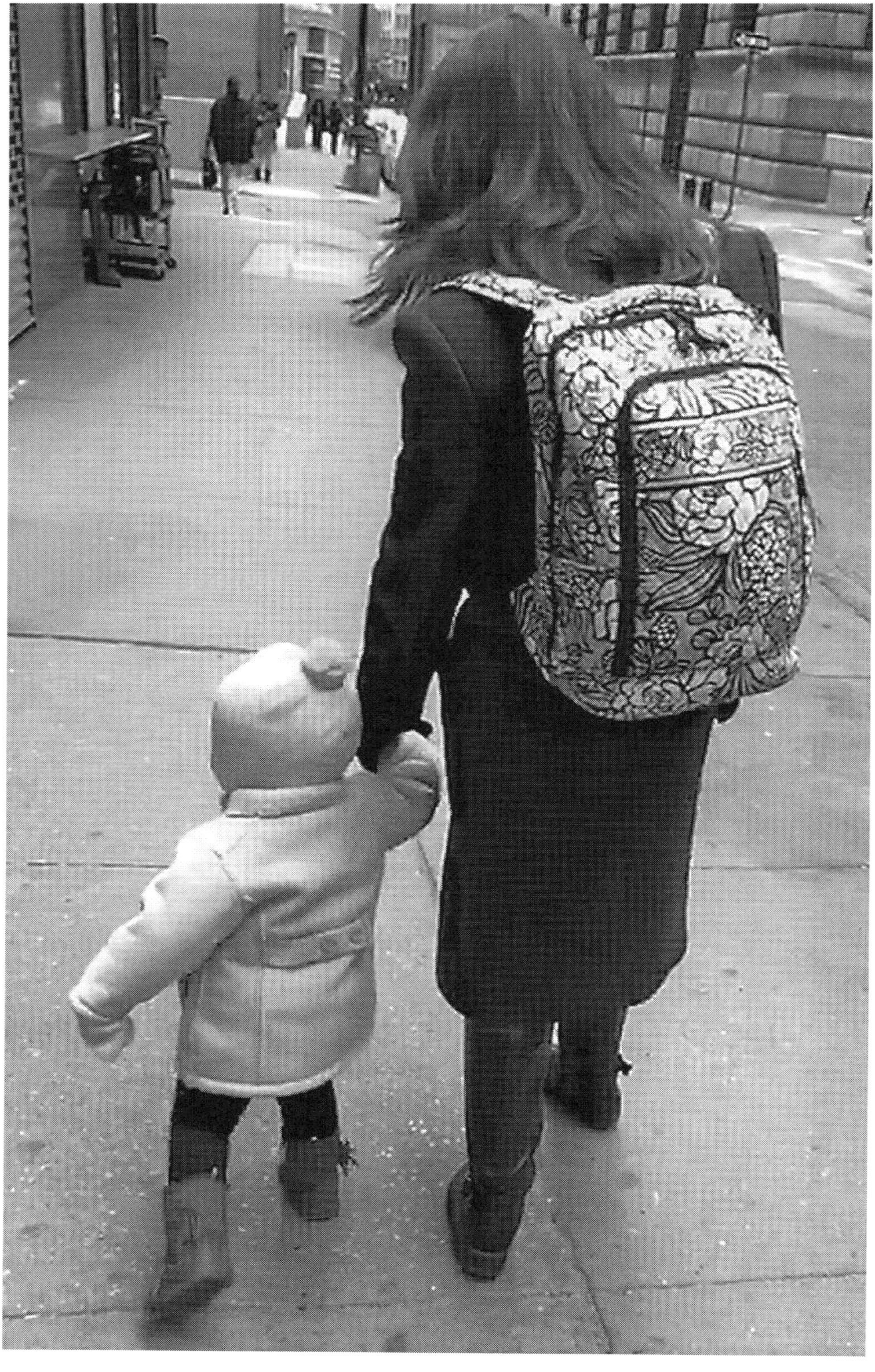

•

She found the difference

Between youth and adulthood

To be cruel in nature

For in youth

We are careless and break things

By accident

As adults

We care less

And break them on purpose

• • •
Broken Footprints Faded Hearts

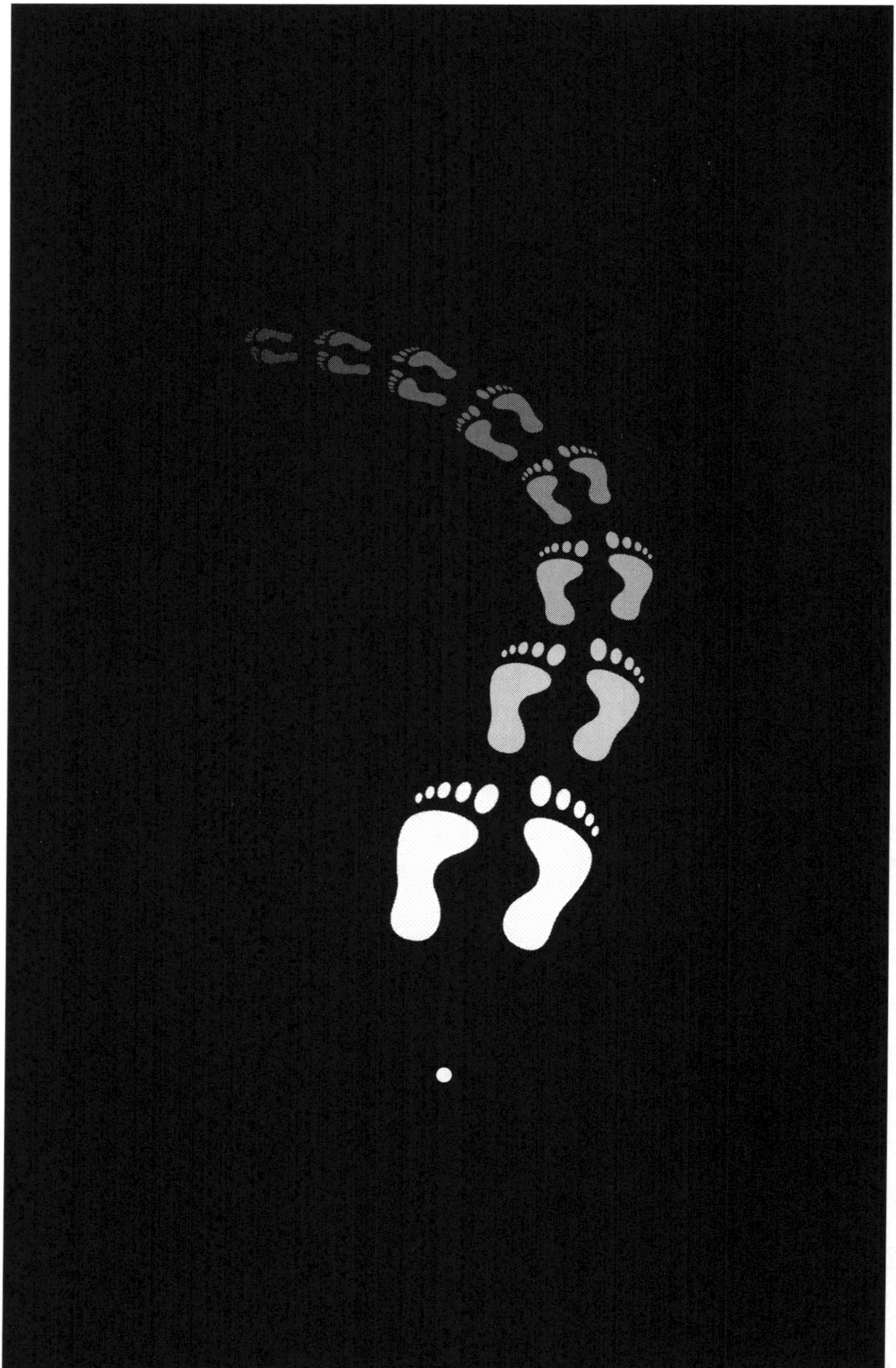

She tried to build a life upon weak men,

Whose foundations shifted like sand.

But in the rubble of those fragile

And collapsed ruins,

She found the rocks necessary

To build her foundation anew;

Strong, unshakable, and true

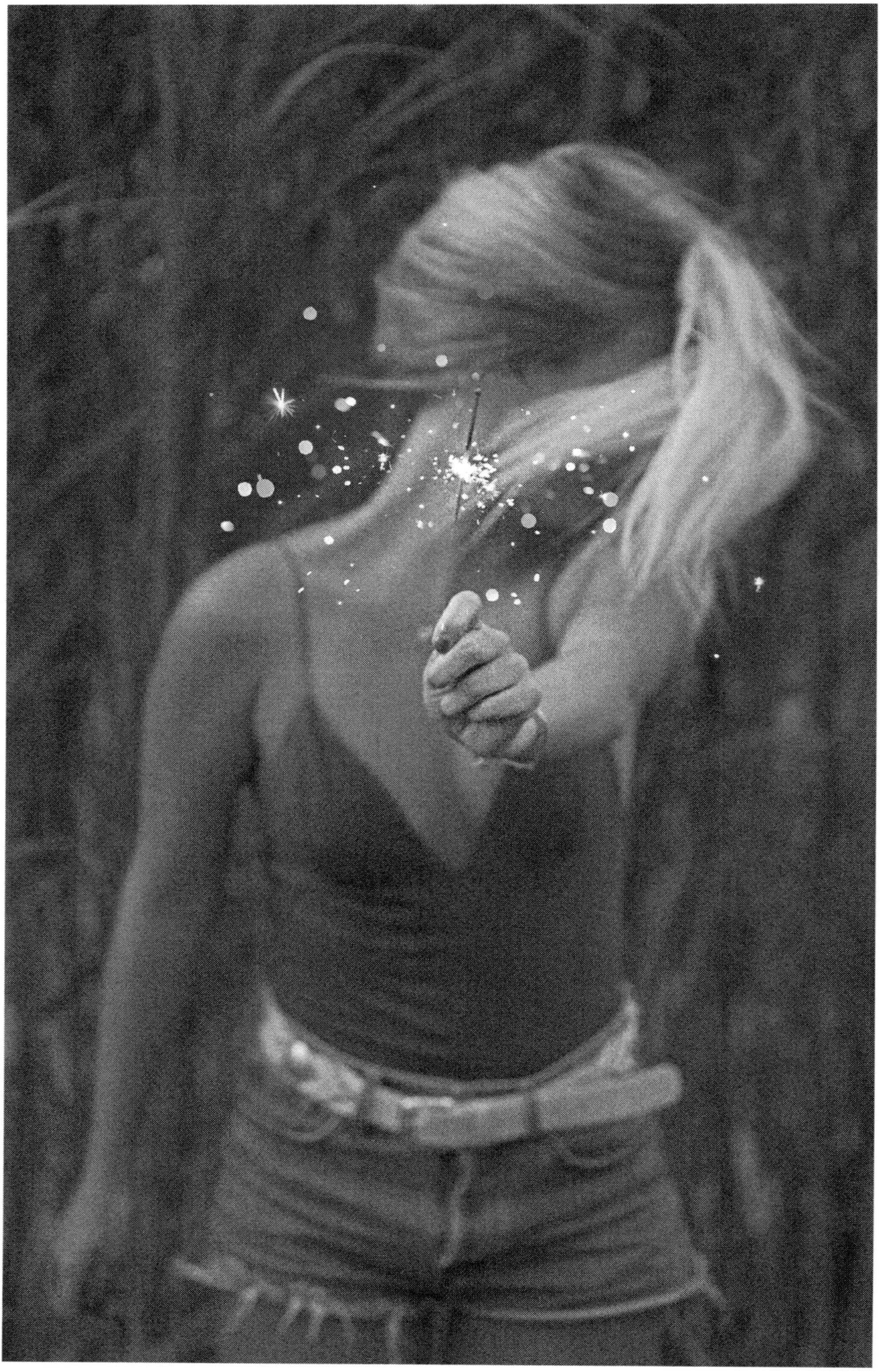

●

He tried encasing her in glass,

As if he could bottle fire

Without extinguishing

The flame

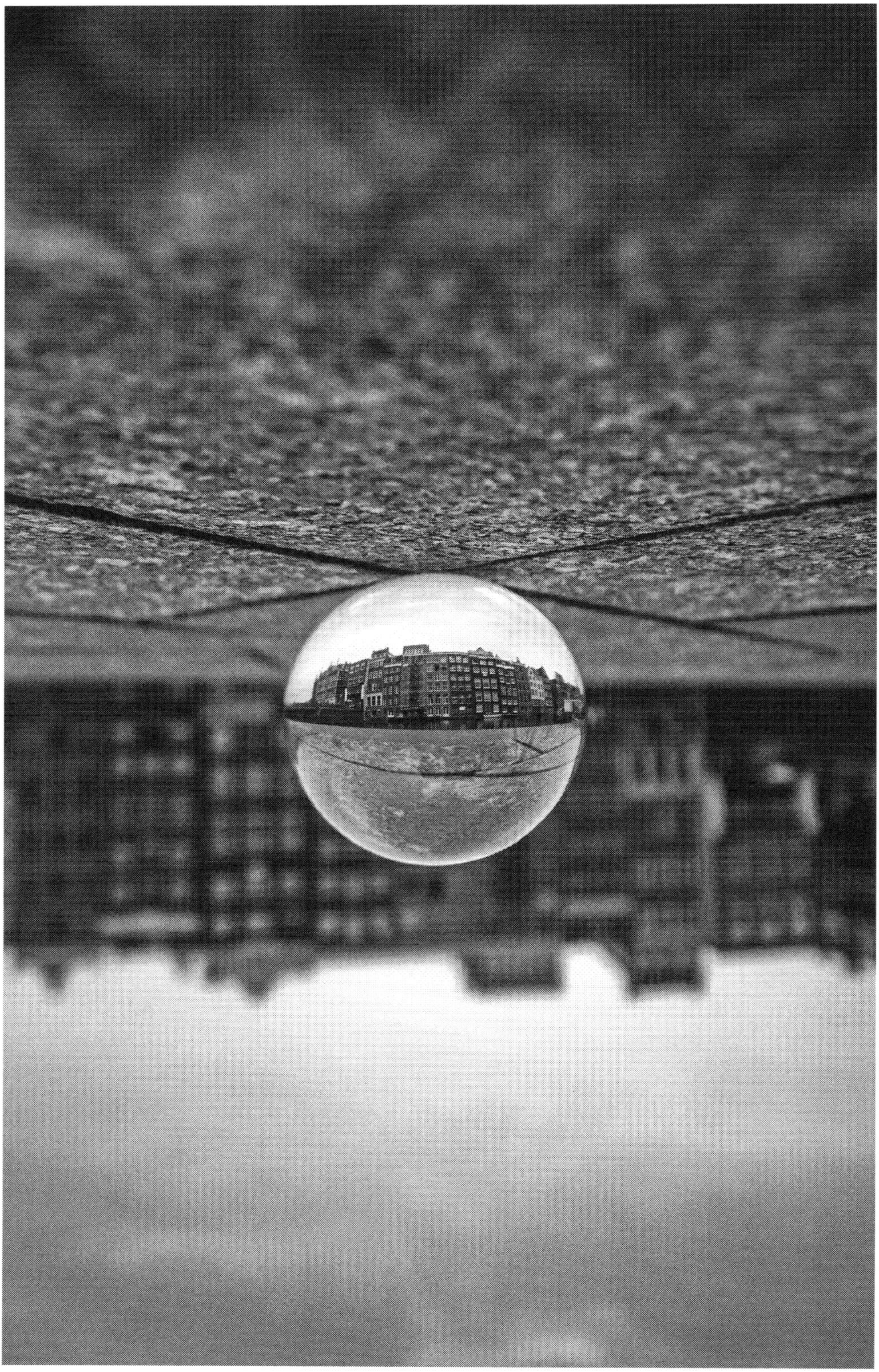

•

The asylum gate

Lies wrenched and open

The crazy be out and free

Oh what a world

It shall be

• • •
Broken Footprints Faded Hearts

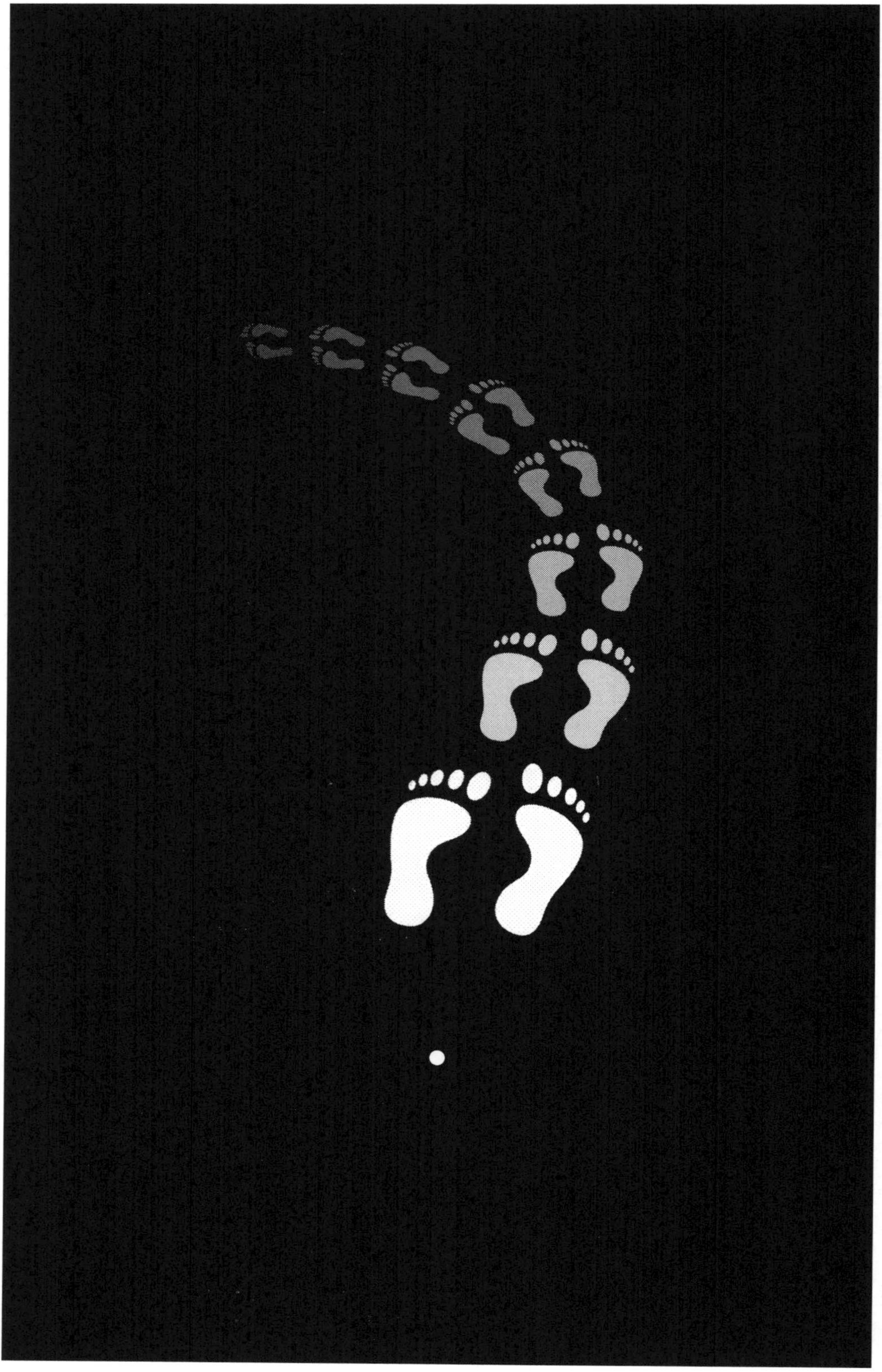

The thing about saving people is that

They must be willing to save themselves

As well.

And the best people will try,

With everything they have,

To save themselves

If it means

Saving the ones they love

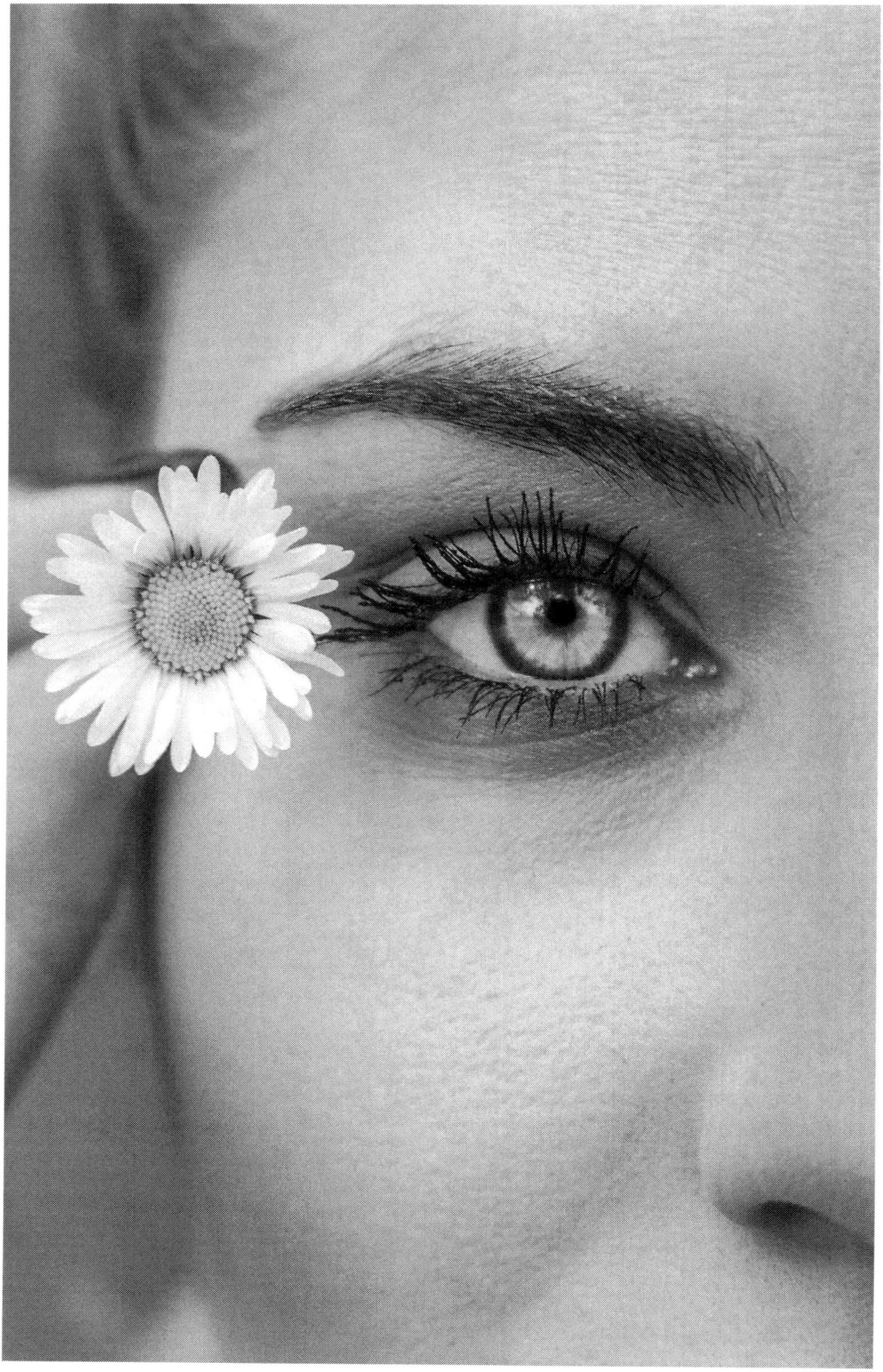

●

Don't pluck daisies

Just because

You can

• • •
Broken Footprints Faded Hearts

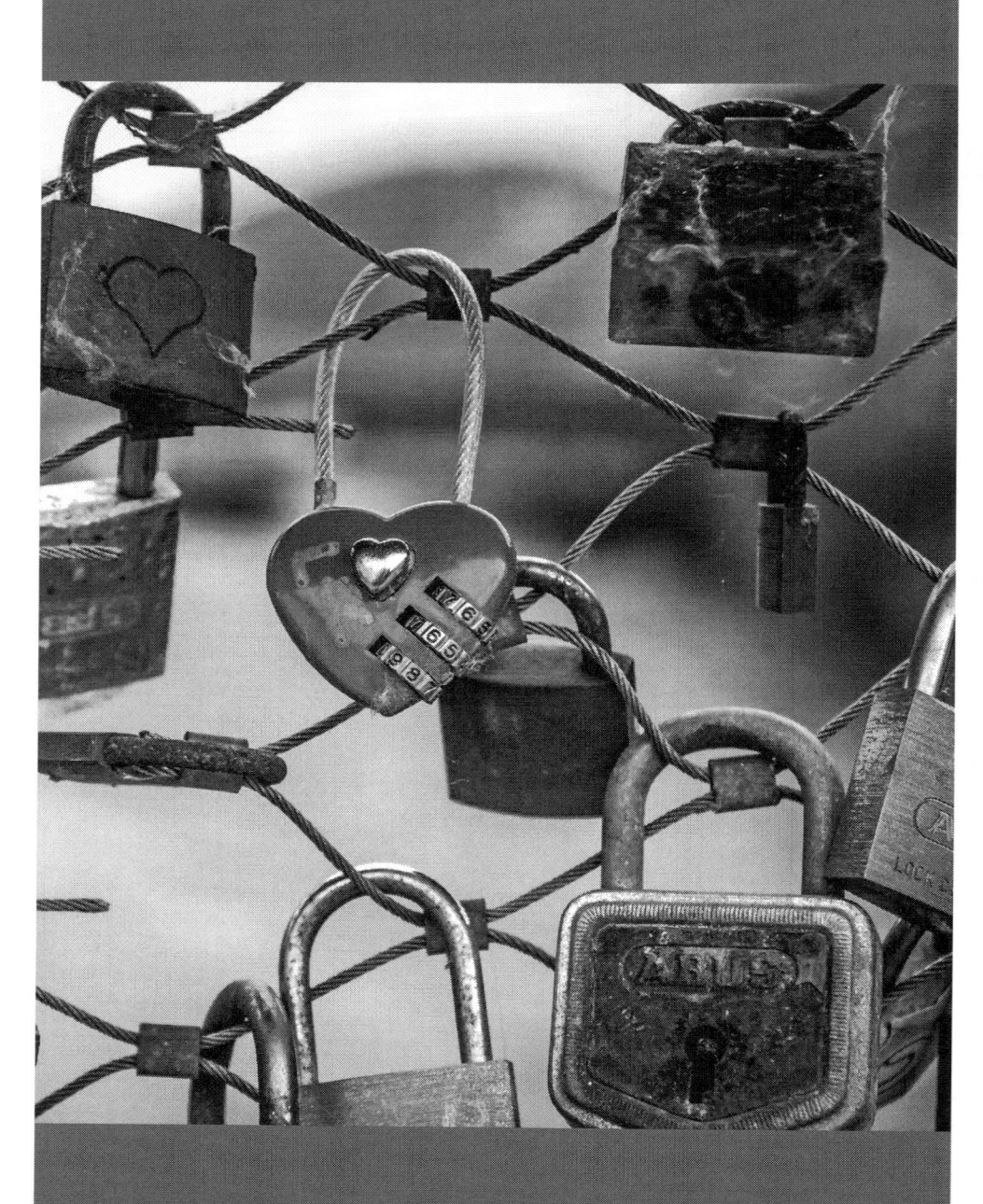

●

Invisible chains are the worst,

There is no hole and no key

A strong heart

And will

And strain

Are the only ways

We eventually

Break ourselves free

• • •
Broken Footprints Faded Hearts

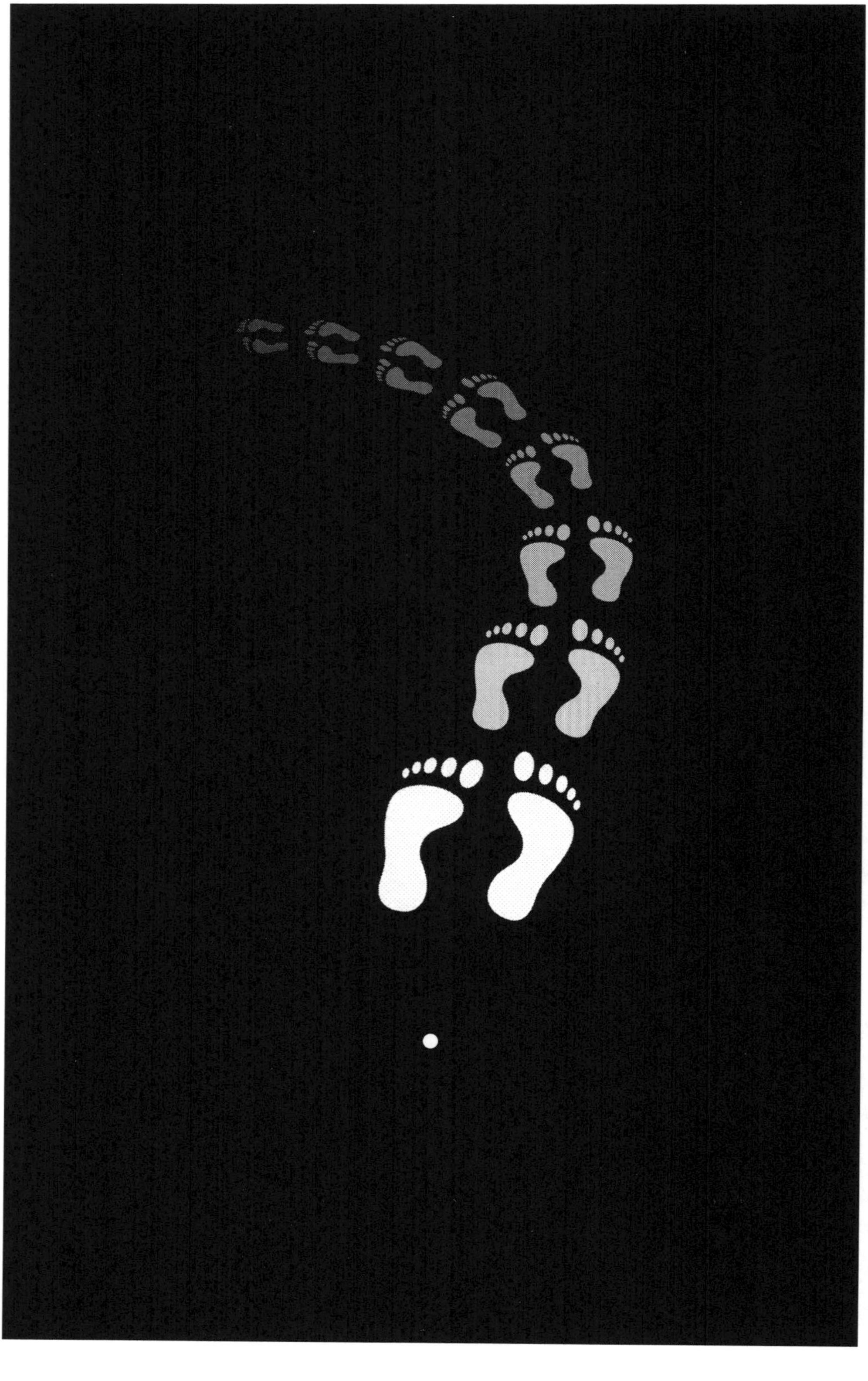

•

She wasn't born cold.

But she knows to keep her hopes on ice.

Rotting dreams

Are no way to grow old.

Flash-frozen can be revived.

Hopes can thaw another day.

But today she keeps a chill.

It's how things

Left for dead

Survive instead

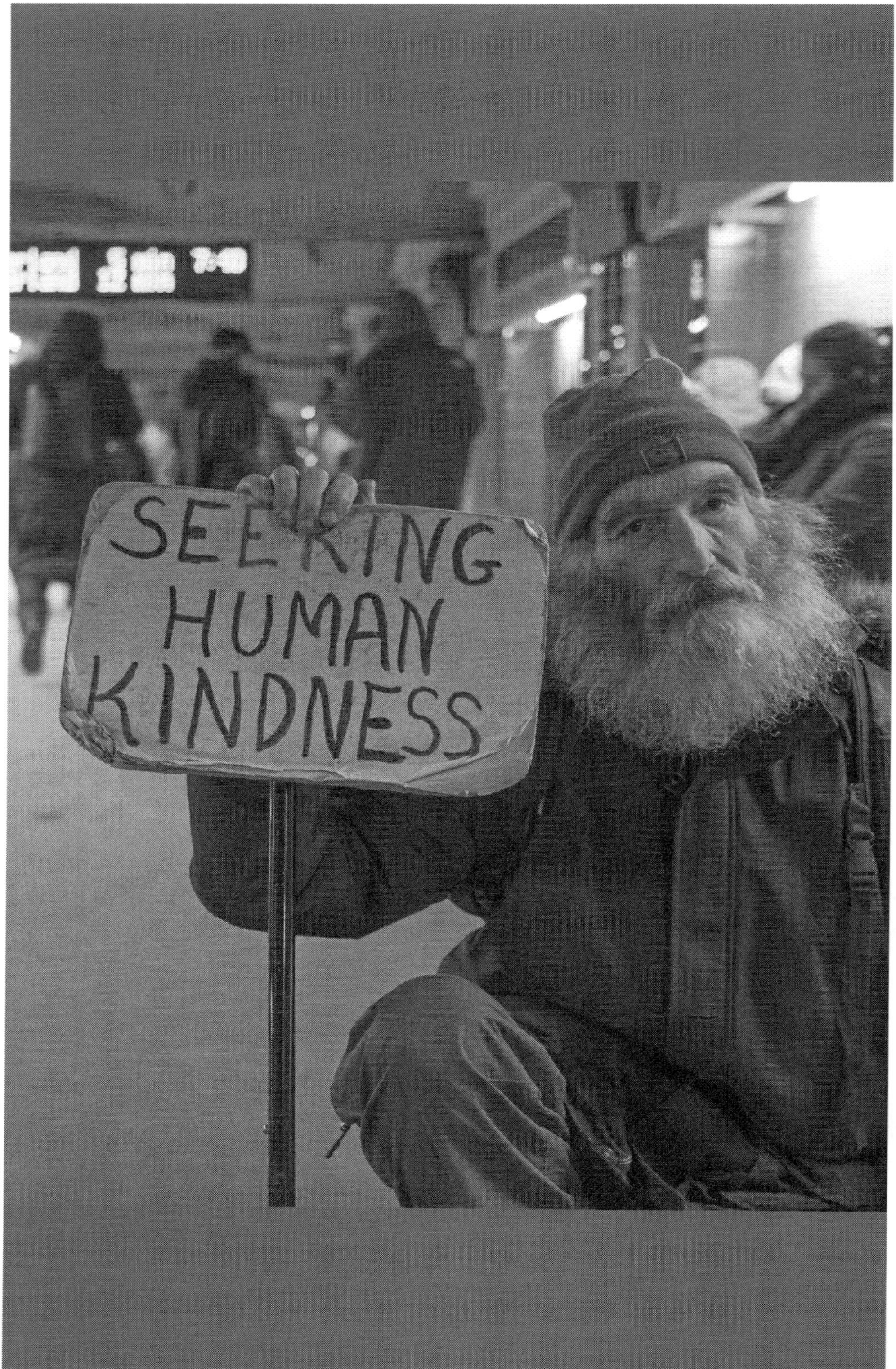
SEEKING
HUMAN
KINDNESS

●

You're not broken.

Your system is just in shock

Because the world is full of assholes

Don't worry.

You'll be angry next

And you should be.

Be okay demanding what is fair and just.

Be okay demanding more

Out of your fellow humans

● ● ●
Broken Footprints Faded Hearts

And when our hearts do break,

It won't be cuz of some violent

Earthquake, but rather when we

Softly walk away,

A whisper never uttered,

Or a pledge of forever

Taken back day by day

•

It's funny how humans are never really content.

We hate not being seen, but more than that

We fear having nowhere to hide.

To be seen completely, as we are,

Is where our true terror lies.

And unfortunately, if we reveal only pieces of

Ourselves, our Greater Self longs to be seen

As well. And it will be. So better to take the

Leap, at least, in the direction of your choice

And hope that the rocks below are covered

By a warm net of love, understanding,

Compassion, and unchecked empathy

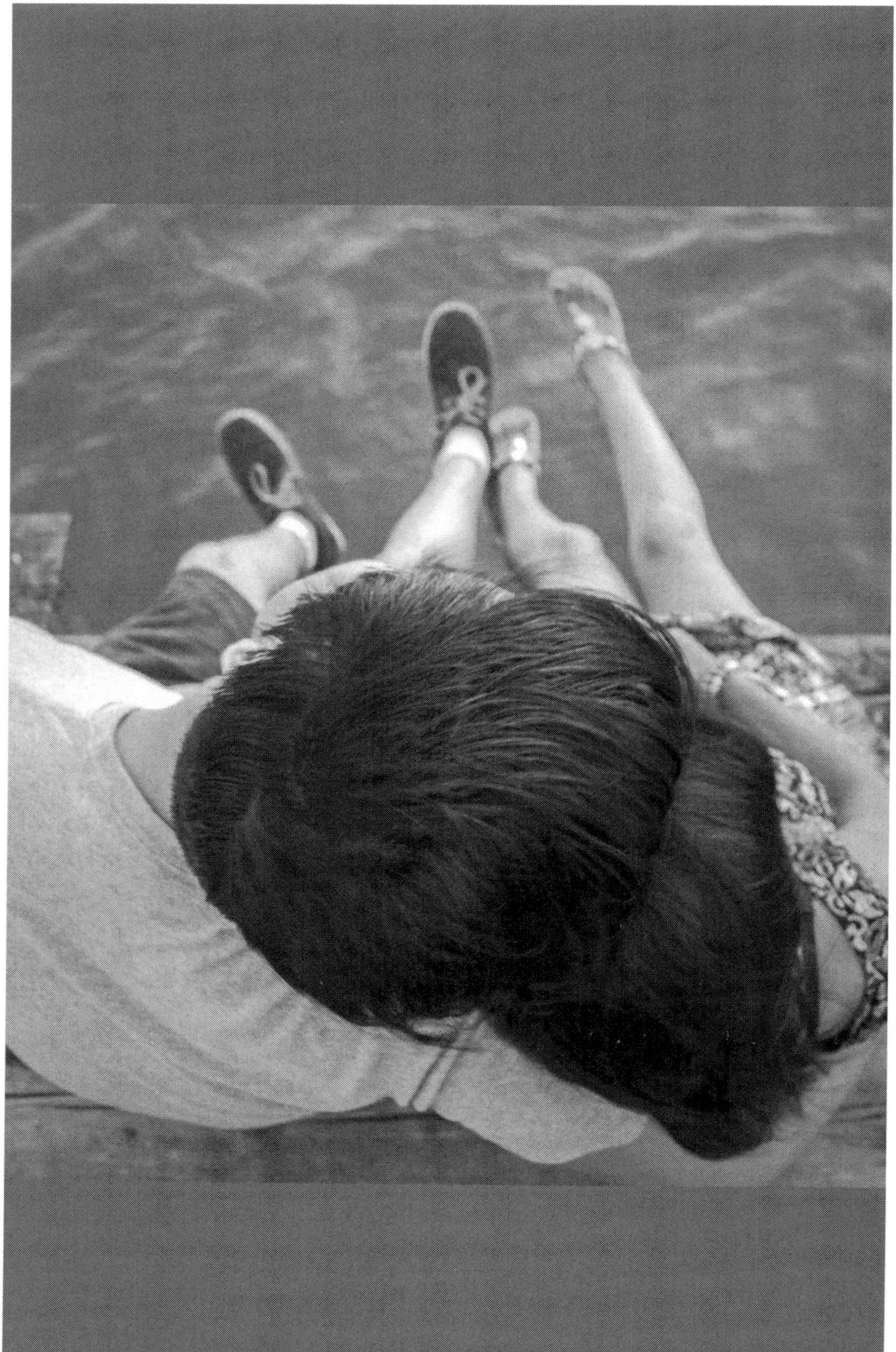

•

She just needed to know
That she was enough. So I
Thought of how she was so
Much more than enough. She
Was my minute, my hour,
My day. She was my universe,
My world, and my home. But
I said none of that. I just let
Her cry, and let my arm be
There to hold shaking shoulders
Steady. And in that moment,
I only hoped I was enough
For her

• • •

Broken Footprints Faded Hearts

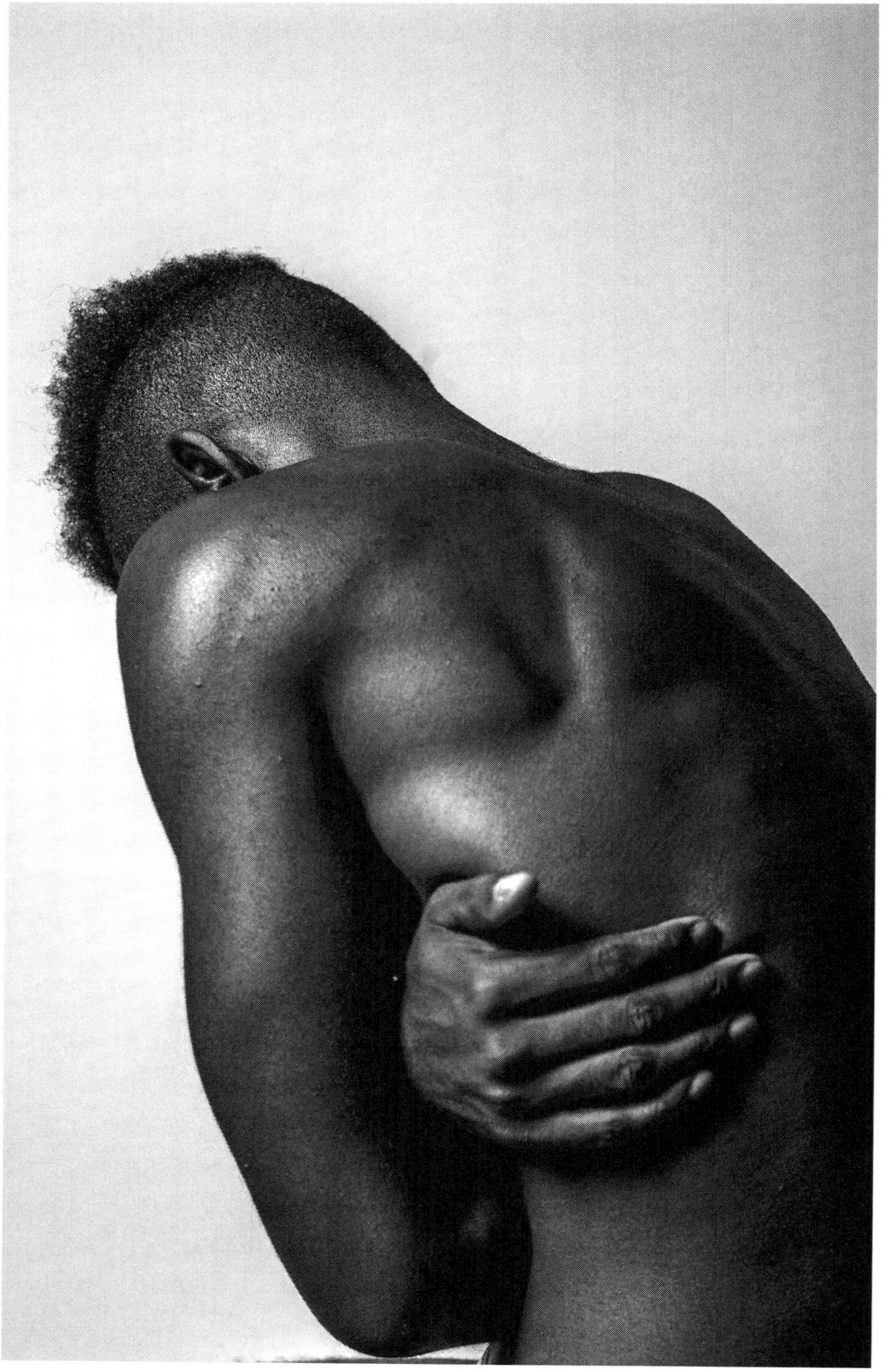

●

You can't be broken

If you were never complete

When the cracks began

• • •
Broken Footprints Faded Hearts

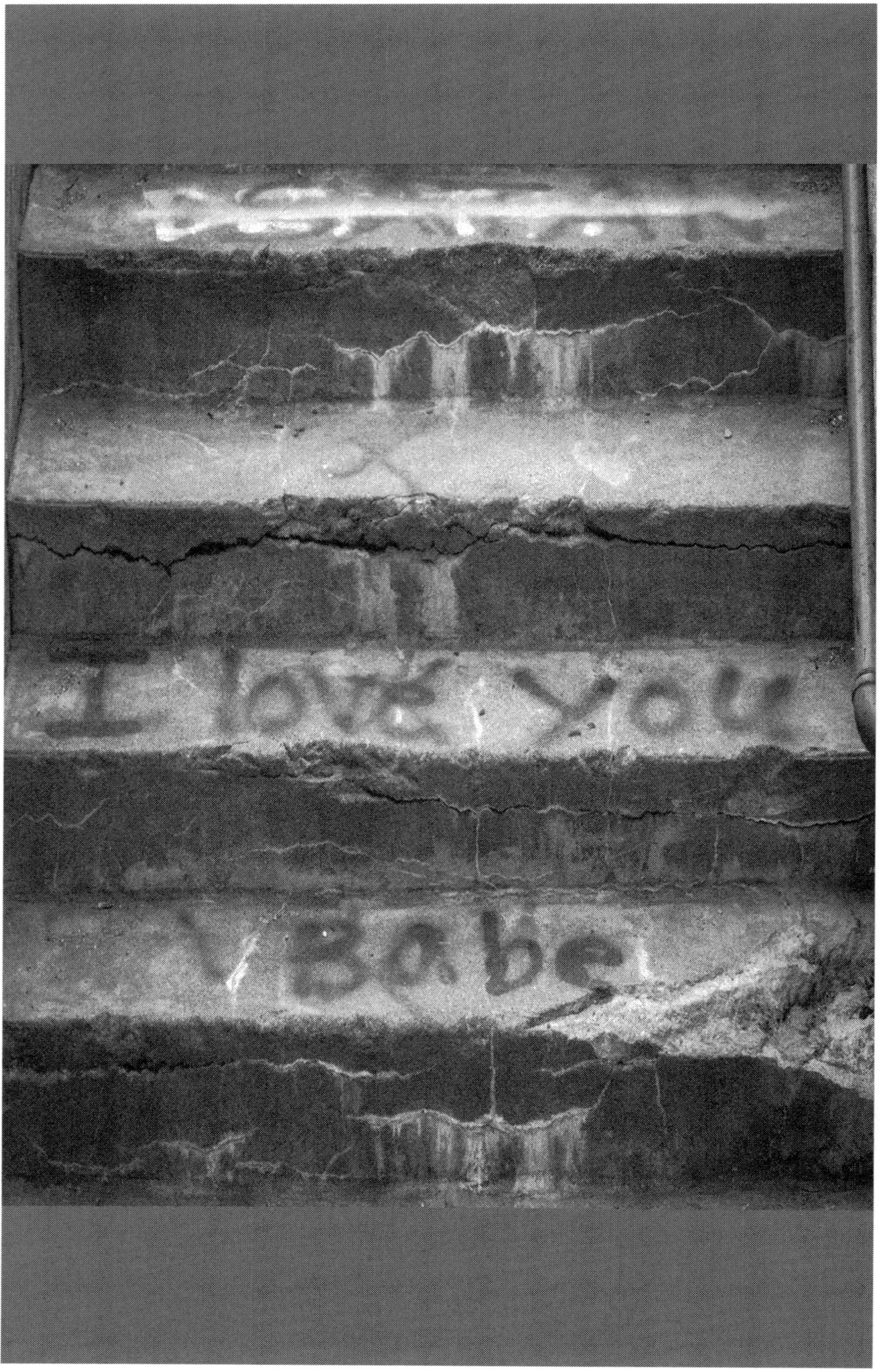
I love You
Babe

•

She doesn't want words without action.

And she doesn't want action without words.

Either can fail her

Through inadequacy or misunderstanding.

Give her your word as well as your

Follow-through.

Your person deserves to have both

• • •
Broken Footprints Faded Hearts

●

She's just tired of waiting for you

To figure it out. She's sad because

She figured you out ages ago

And still wasted all that time

Waiting for the "you"

That never showed

He told her everything

A million times

The things she wished

He'd have shown her

Just for once

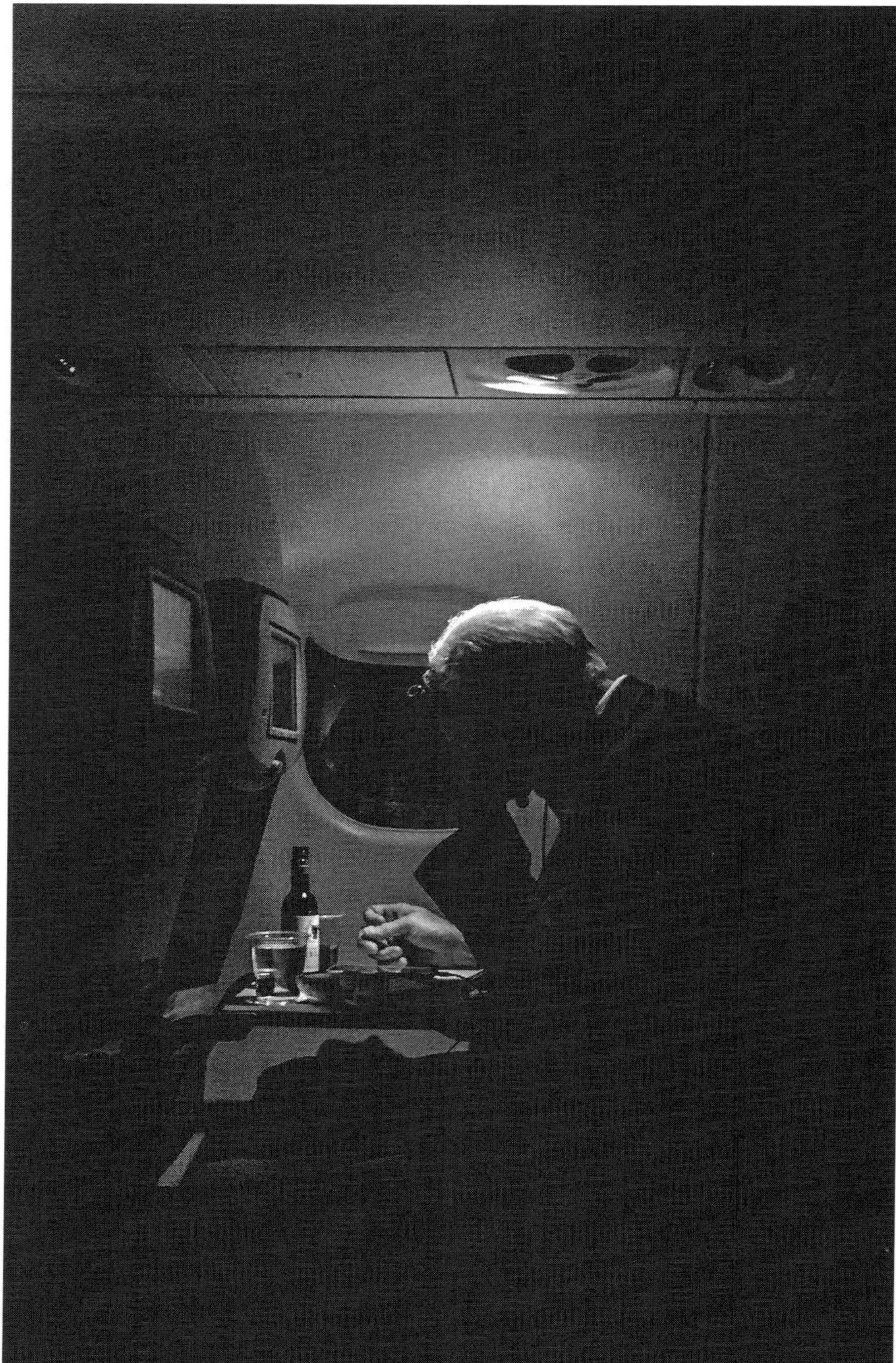

●

Somewhere, she has the same moon as me

Though, perhaps a slightly different view.

Or her day connects to night

Across the sea

And her thoughts follow constellations

Back to me

But if the stars don't prove true,

And tonight we cannot be,

Please quick sleep come to me

Because a dream will have to do

● ● ●
Broken Footprints Faded Hearts

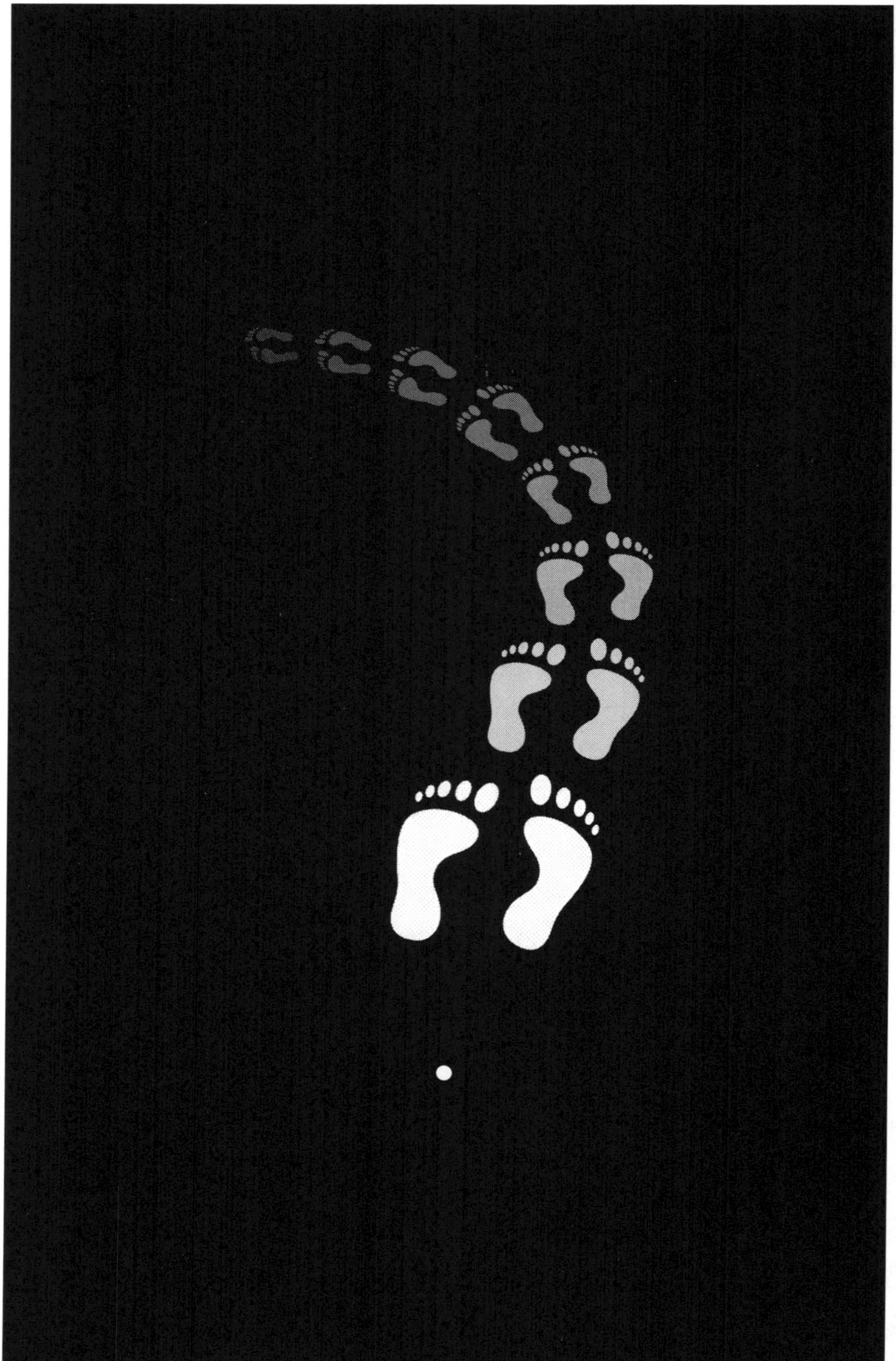

•

She did all she could

And it was never enough

For him.

But one day

It was enough

For her

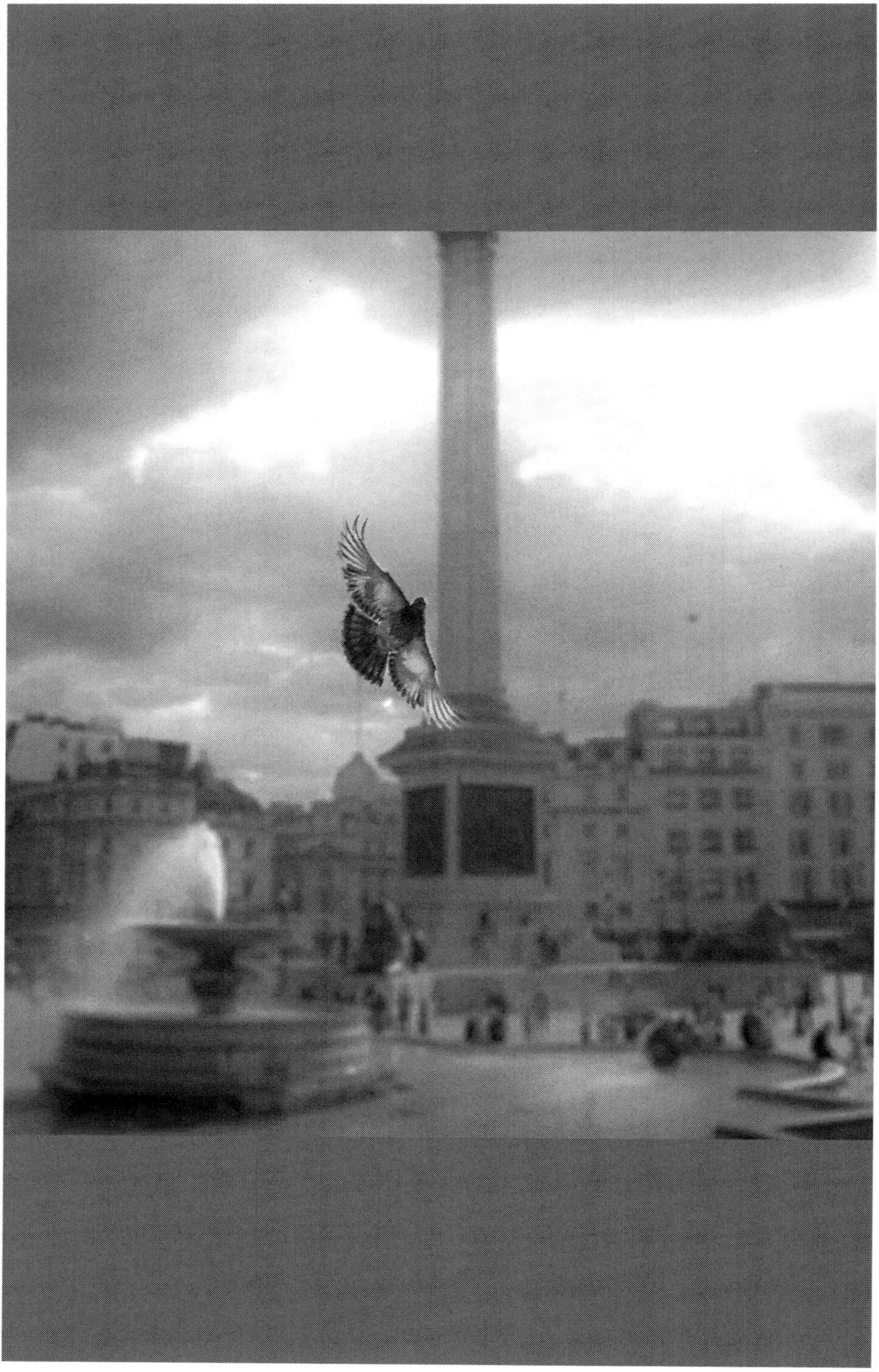

It's just me and your locket

With a picture as faded as the memory

Of our happy days. If only I could

Keep time in my pocket, I'm sure

I'd find the secret that made us go

Our separate ways. But I never was

Too good at catching things, maybe

That's why you grew them wings

And couldn't stay. It's not fair

That you can't wish upon a locket

For just one more day. But magic died

For me when I didn't say what I

Should've said that day

You finally went away

• • •
Broken Footprints Faded Hearts

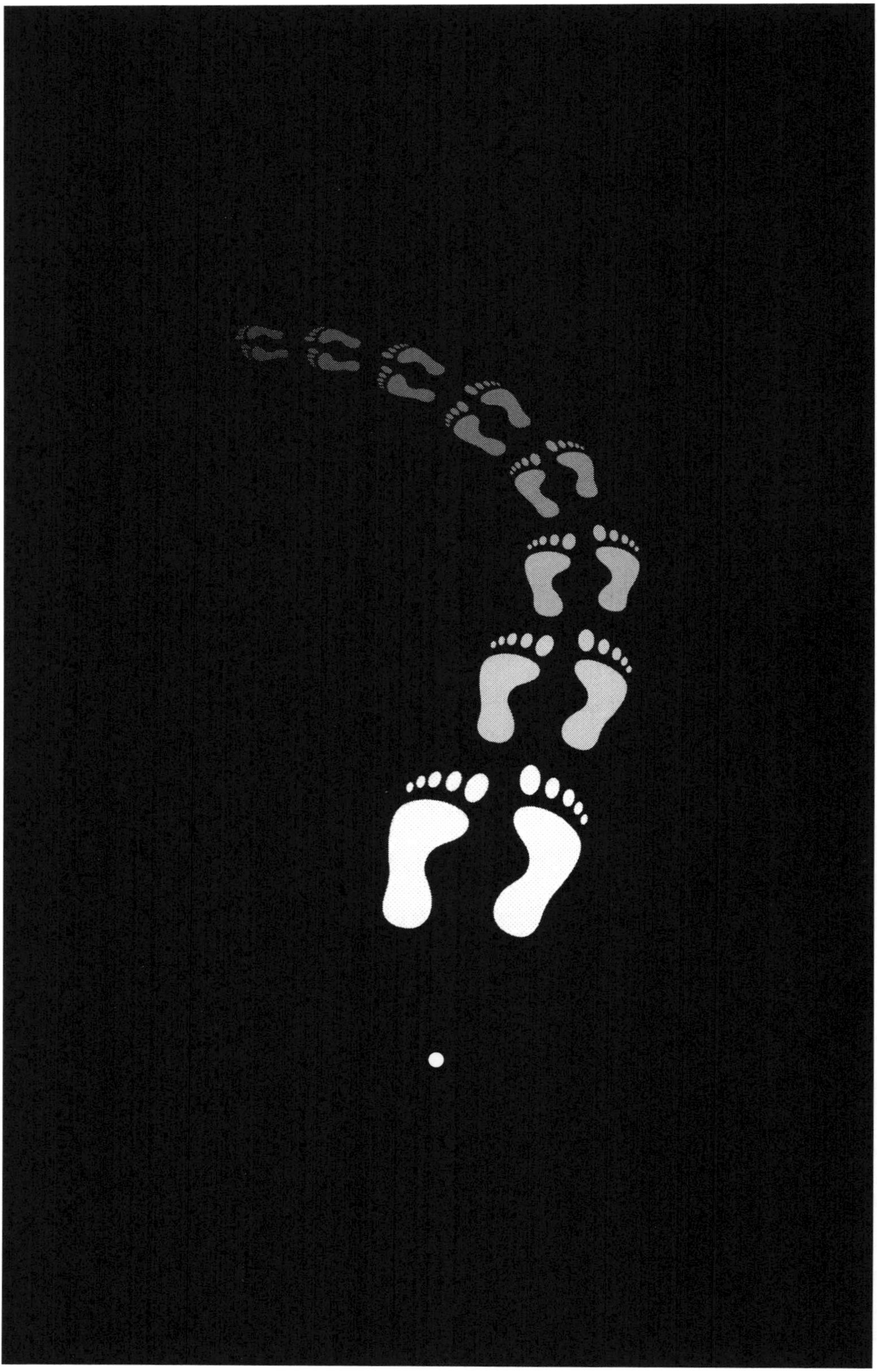

●

This may be

The way the world

And its end meet

With a bang

Begun from

An old man's

Tweet

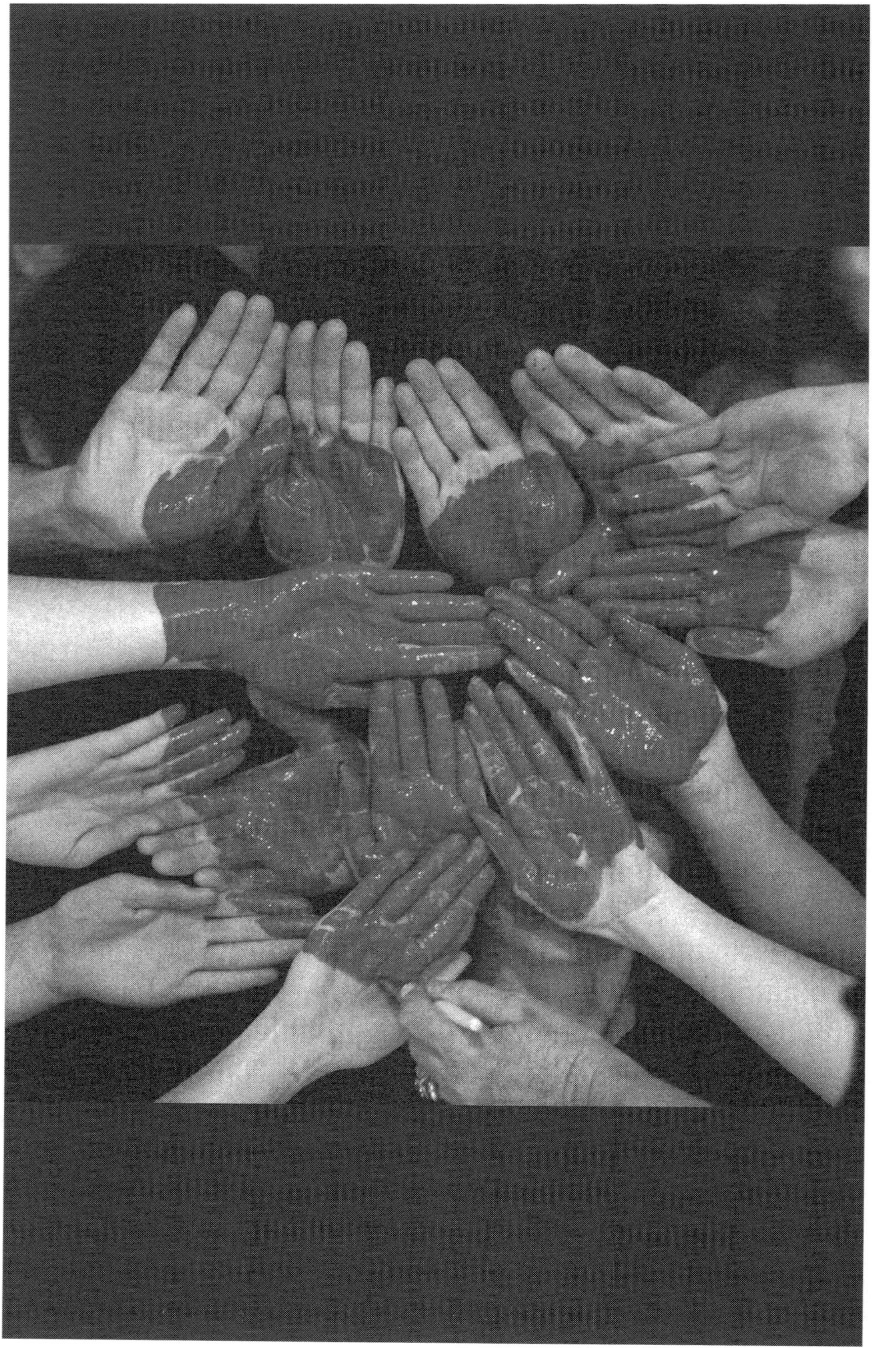

●

The woman guards

Her heart

Because the girl

Suffers thieves

● ● ●
Broken Footprints Faded Hearts

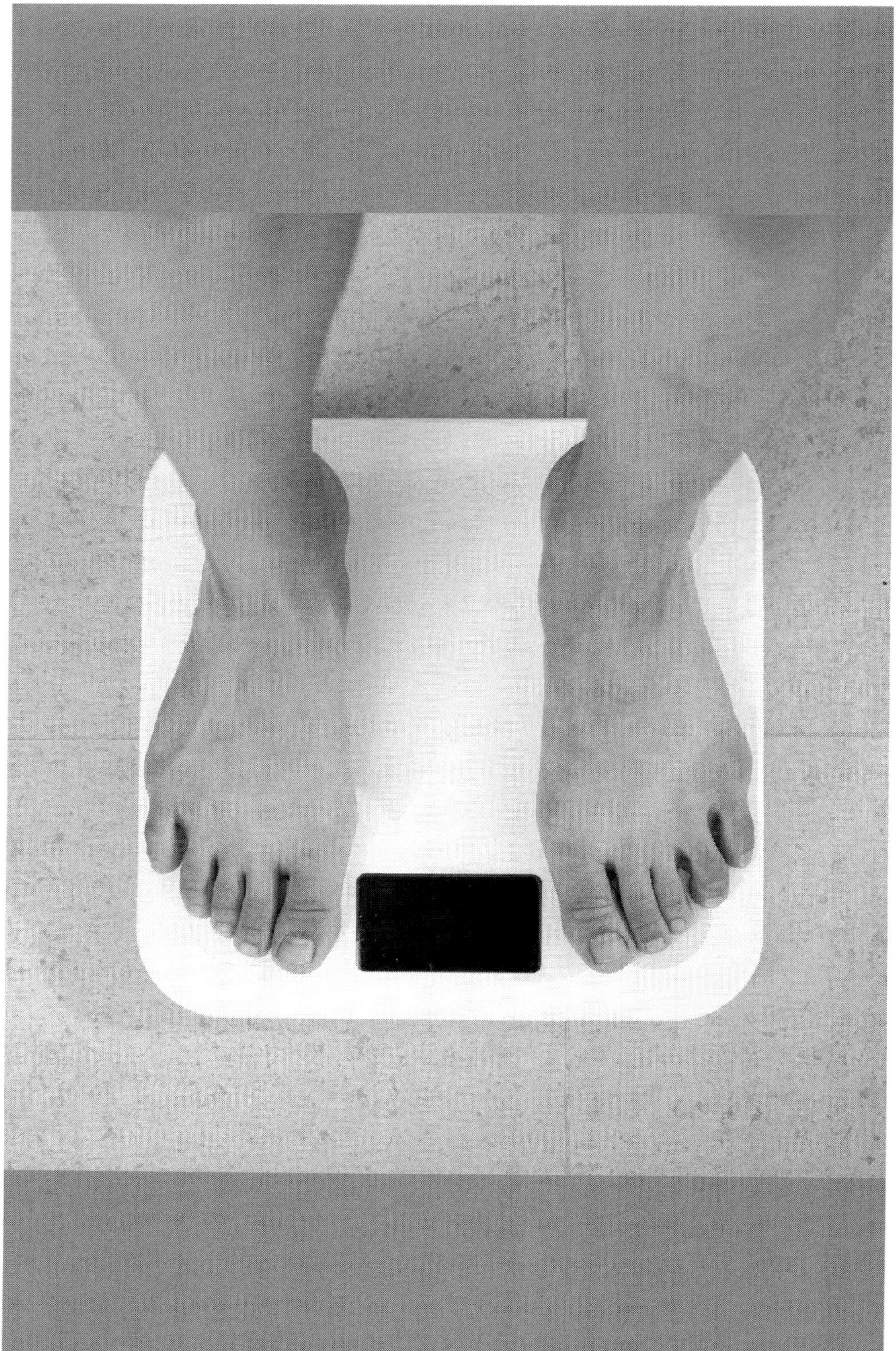

●

Beauty can't be weighed

And yet we give weight

To the weight of so many

Beautiful people

Trying to measure the

Immeasurable for our own

Need to compare things

That are fundamentally

Incomparable

● ● ●
Broken Footprints Faded Hearts

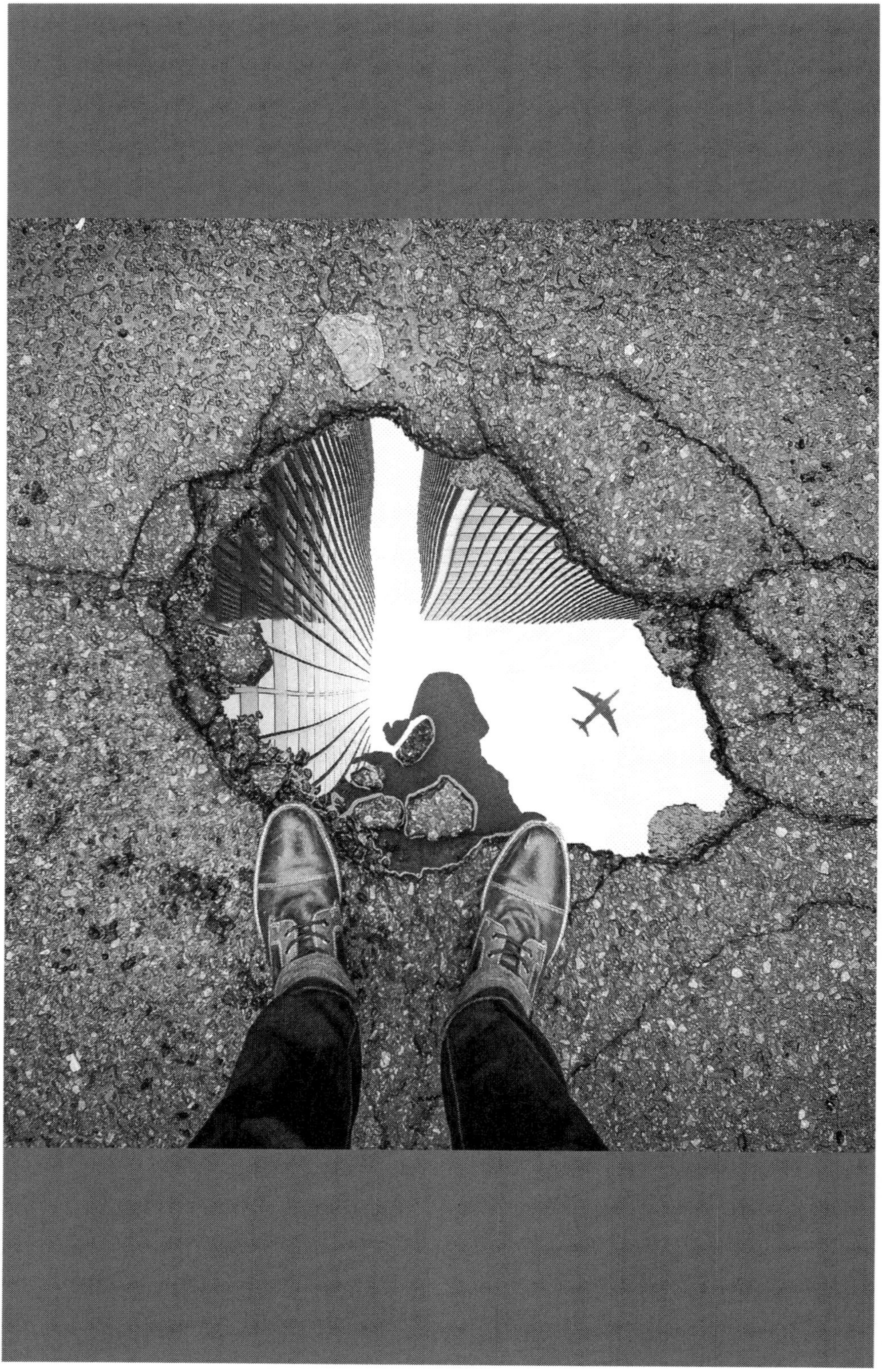

●

In finding yourself

You forget the person

Who was looking to begin with,

Either little by little

Or all at once.

This can be bitter

Or sweet,

For worse

Or for the best,

But what once was,

Shall be put to rest

● ● ●
Broken Footprints Faded Hearts

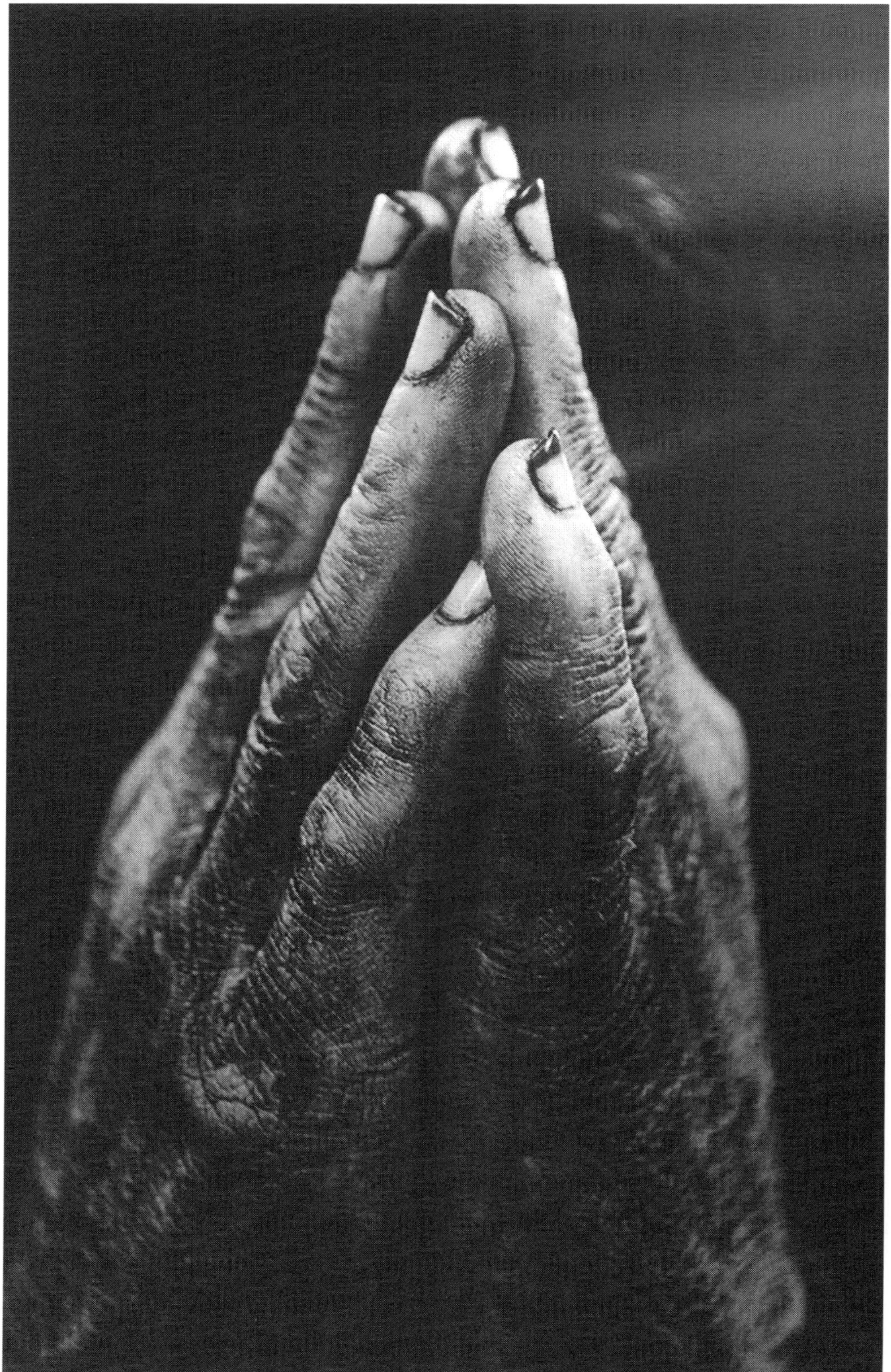

●

She knew

Their dirty hands

Thought her ripe

For plucking

But greedy fingers

Must remember

Pretty flowers often

Carry thorns

• • •
Broken Footprints Faded Hearts

# Us

Us is a collection of memories and ideas about how we can be better. It focuses on how to hold one another up and to create a more open and supportive environment. Largely inspired by the feminist movement of the last year with rallying cries of #MeToo and #ShePersisted, there is a unique opportunity to be a voice where we can champion the cause of equality. This poetry is the perfect forum to lend an additional voice to equality and positivity.

•••
Broken Footprints Faded Hearts

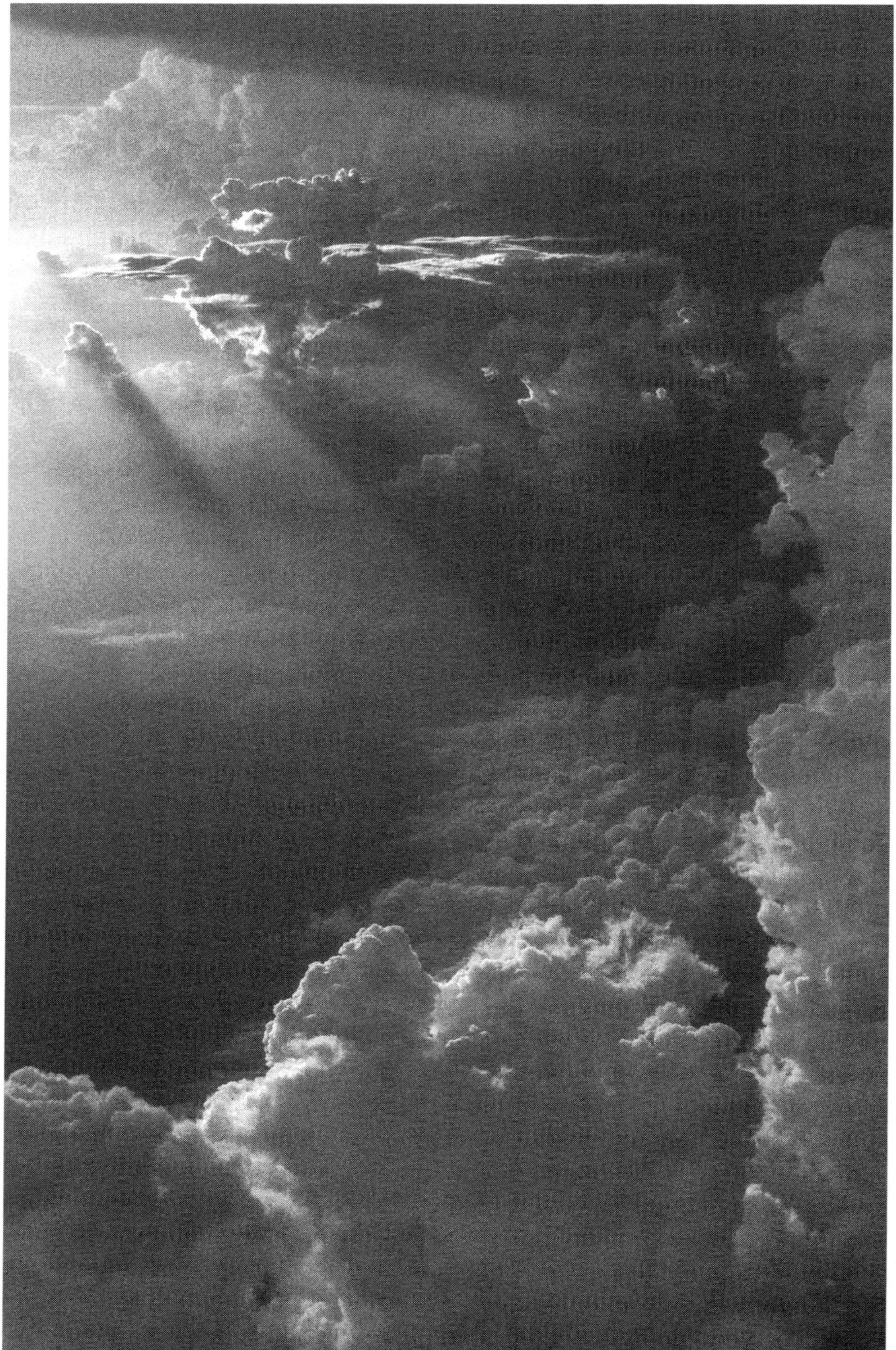

●

I can't dream without you baby;

All the world goes black.

So, let's stay awake a while and

Maybe God will forget to take you back.

Let's watch the sun come up, love.

Cuz if we see it rise, it's just proof

From up above that some days never die.

So, let's spend our time in this endless sun,

Darling, cuz we know it's true.

That of everything there is to do

They were made to do with you

● ● ●
Broken Footprints Faded Hearts

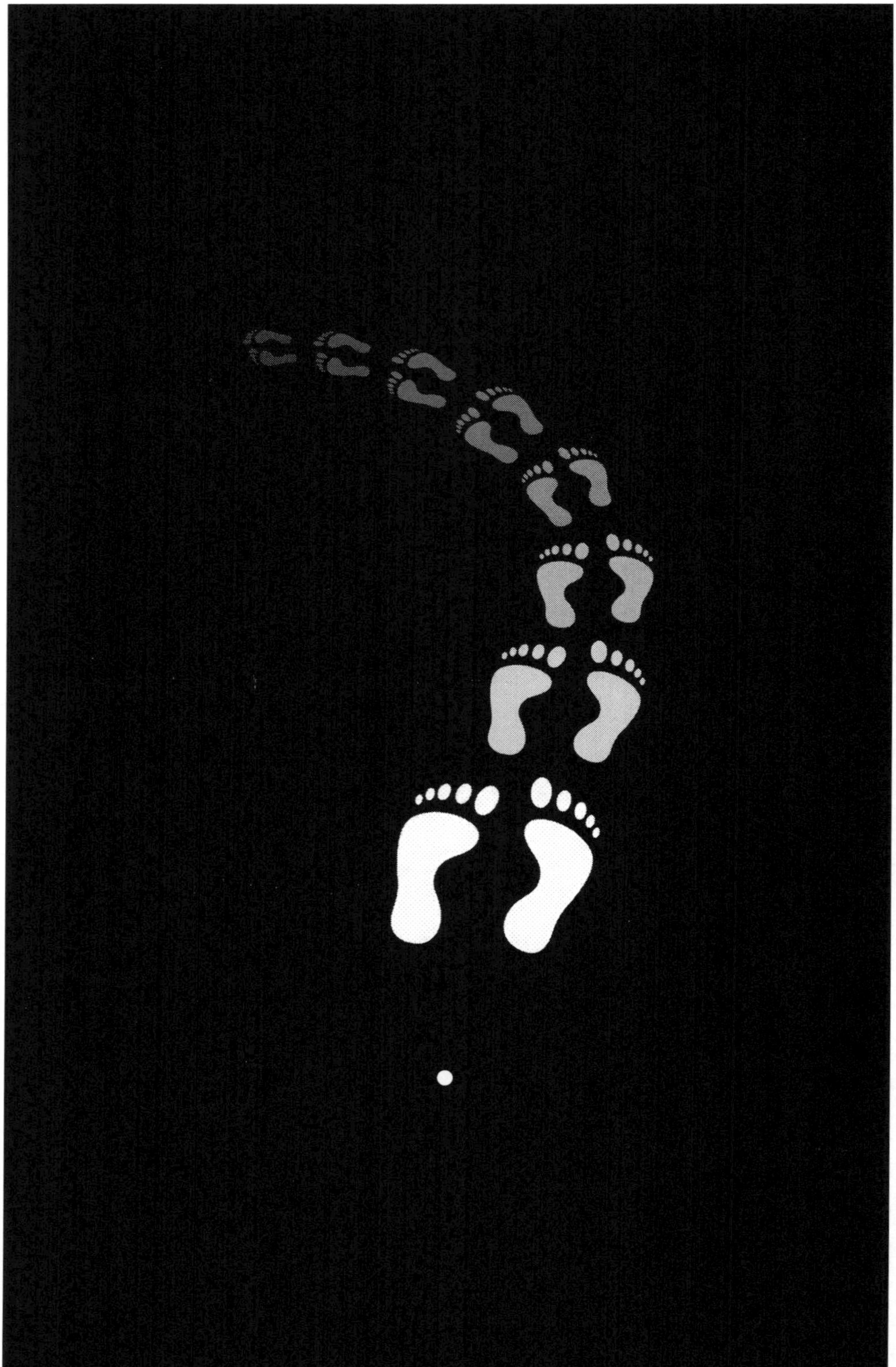

•

Free the love

The world locked

Within her.

It is worth

All the effort

That may take

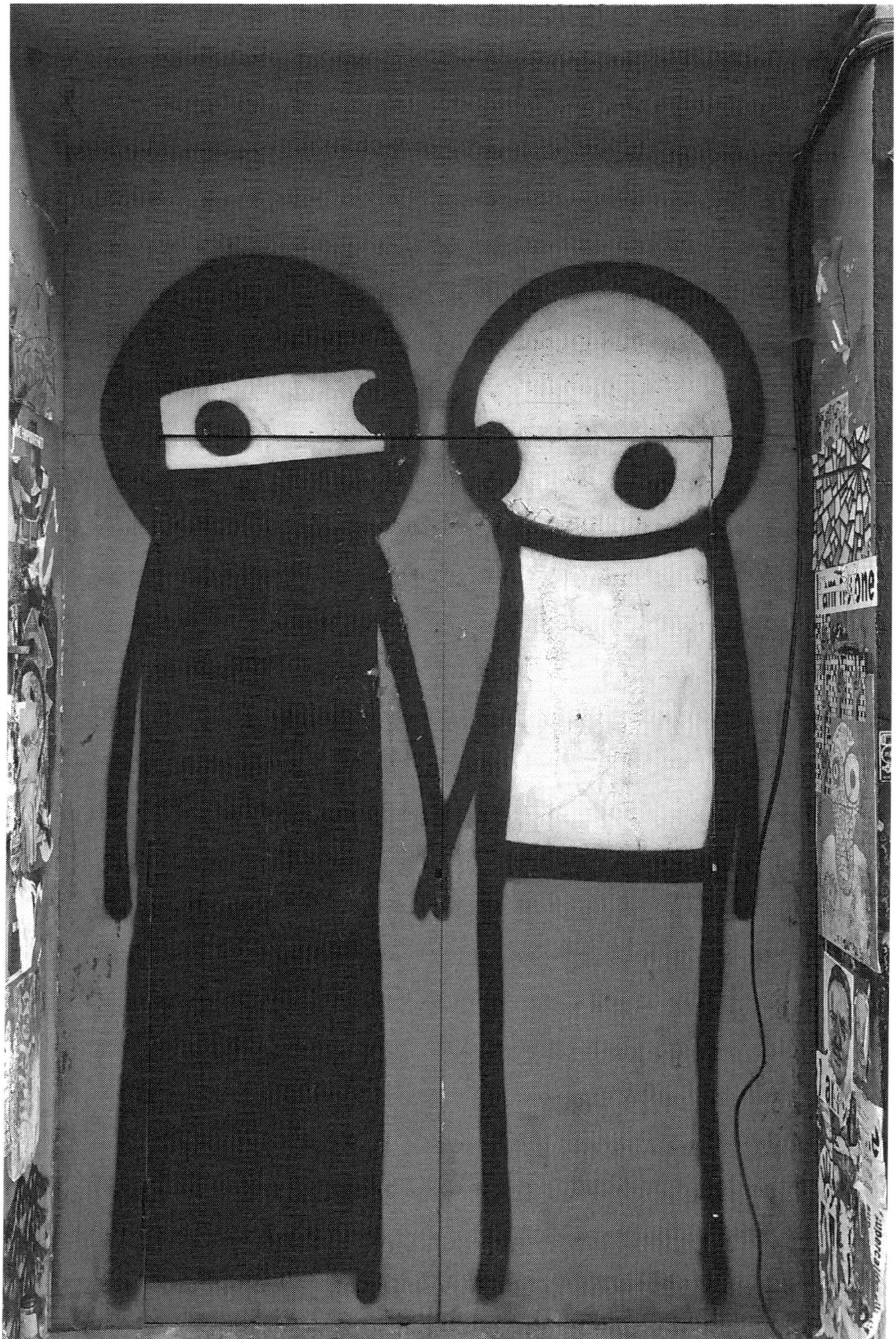

●

The thing is

You said, "I'll be late."

And I knew

No matter what

I'd always

Wait

• • •
Broken Footprints Faded Hearts

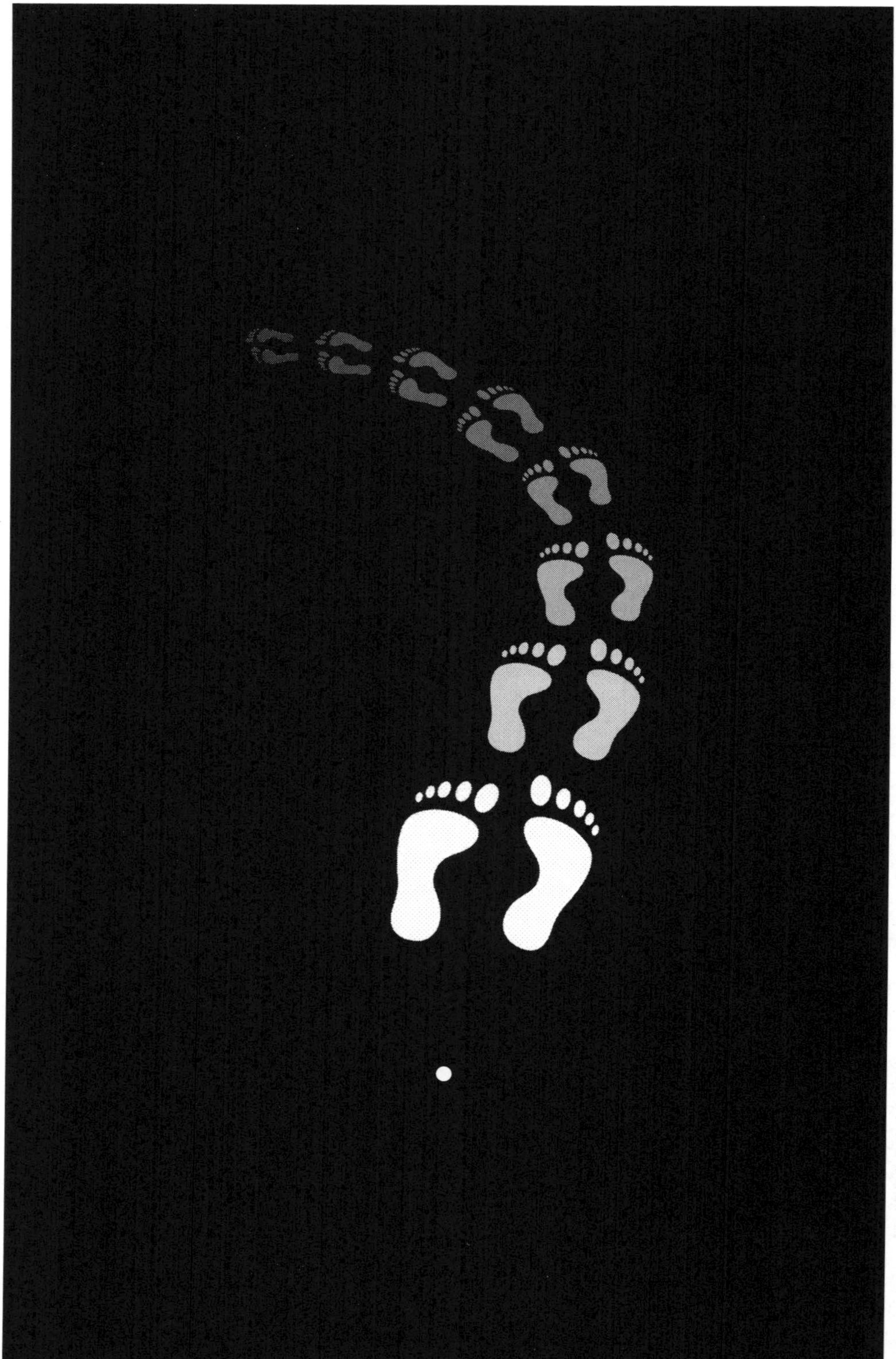

So, she has walls.

Bring a grappling hook.

In the end all she wants

Is to know you did

Whatever it took

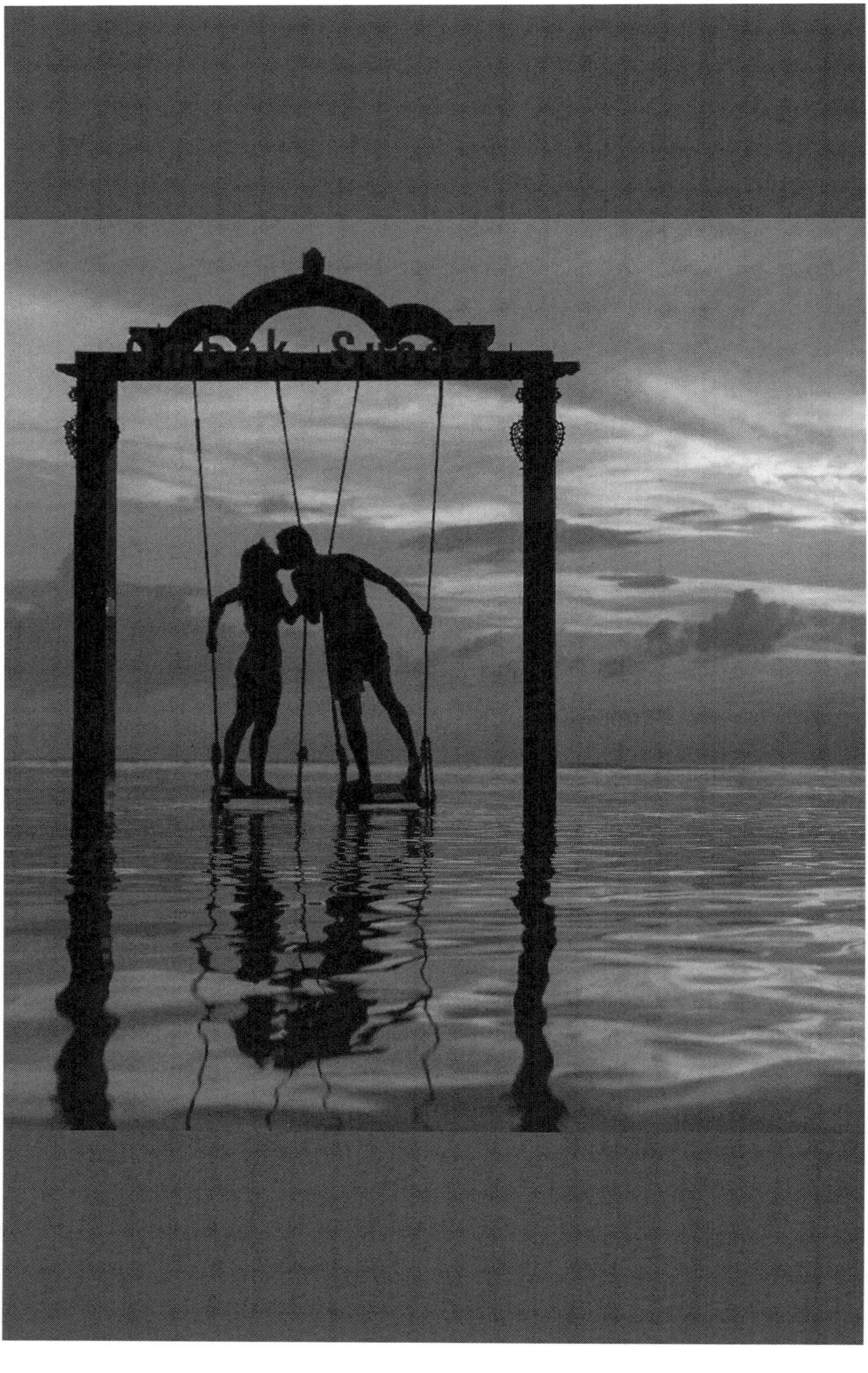

●

She's the beautiful chaos in my life,

The butterfly effect on my soul

From butterfly kisses on my knobby nose.

She's more than a theory.

She's the truth nobody else knows.

She's a secret in my heart

That grows and grows and grows

• • •
Broken Footprints Faded Hearts

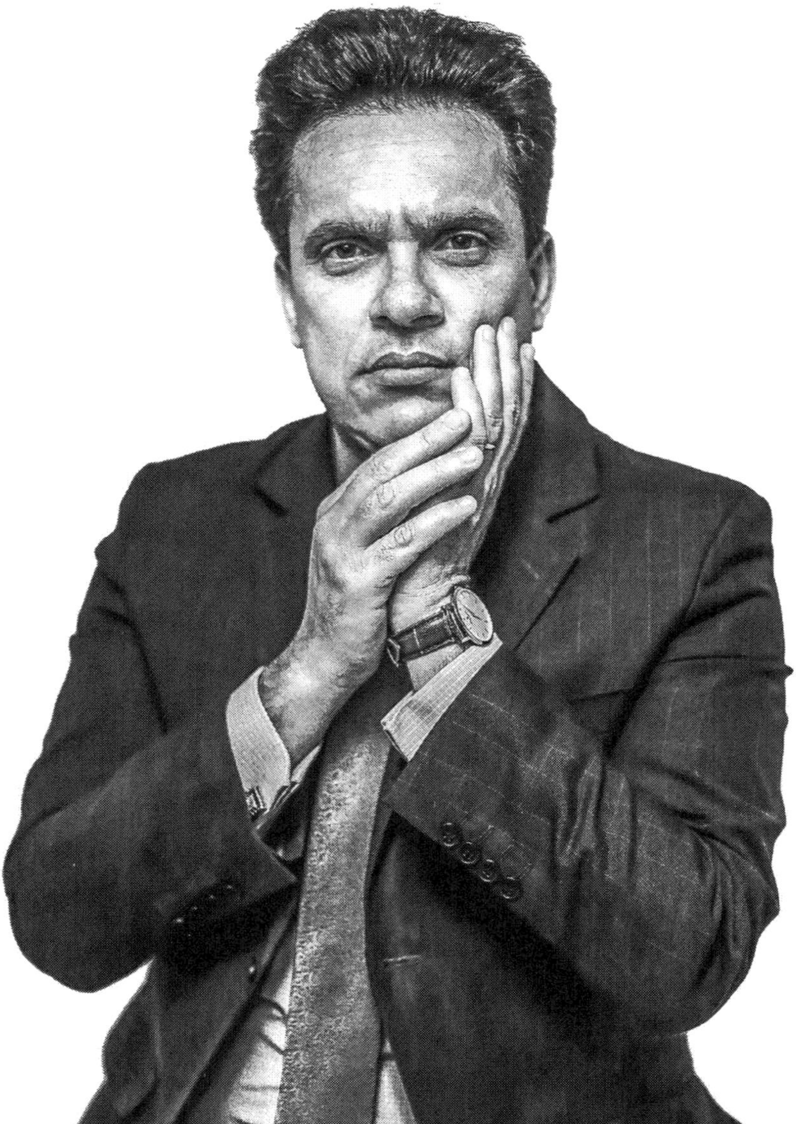

●

My hands

Will treat you gently

Because my fingers

Have felt such pain

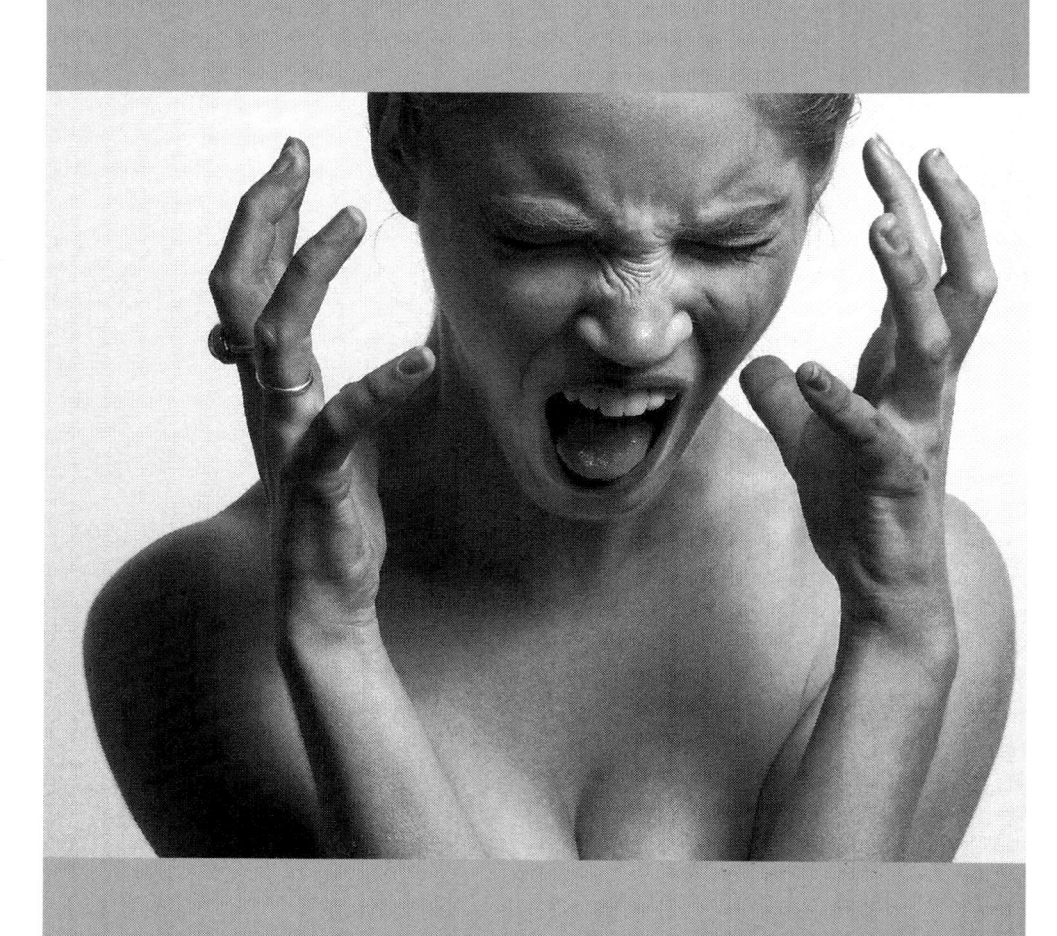

●

She's angry because she has to be.
Ask yourself, "Why?"
Why must she be angry for you
To understand that the status quo
Doesn't work anymore? Instead of
Defending your point of view,
Try and understand hers.
It costs you nothing and has the
Potential to free her from a prison
Of anger where, I promise you,
She doesn't want to be

● ● ●
Broken Footprints Faded Hearts

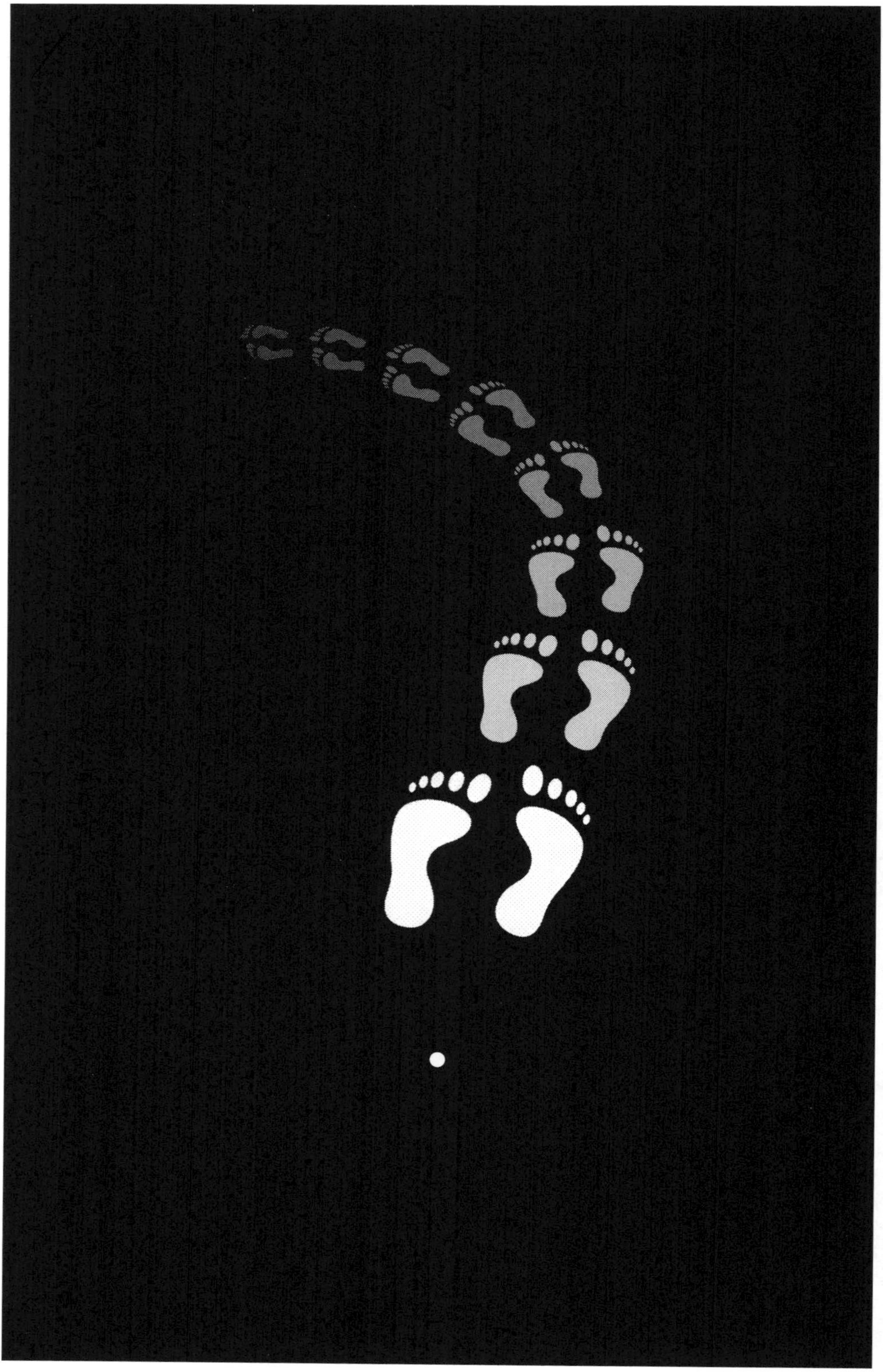

•

Weak people fear

Wild things. And she

Never once gave away

Her freedom for

The safety of

Someone else's dream

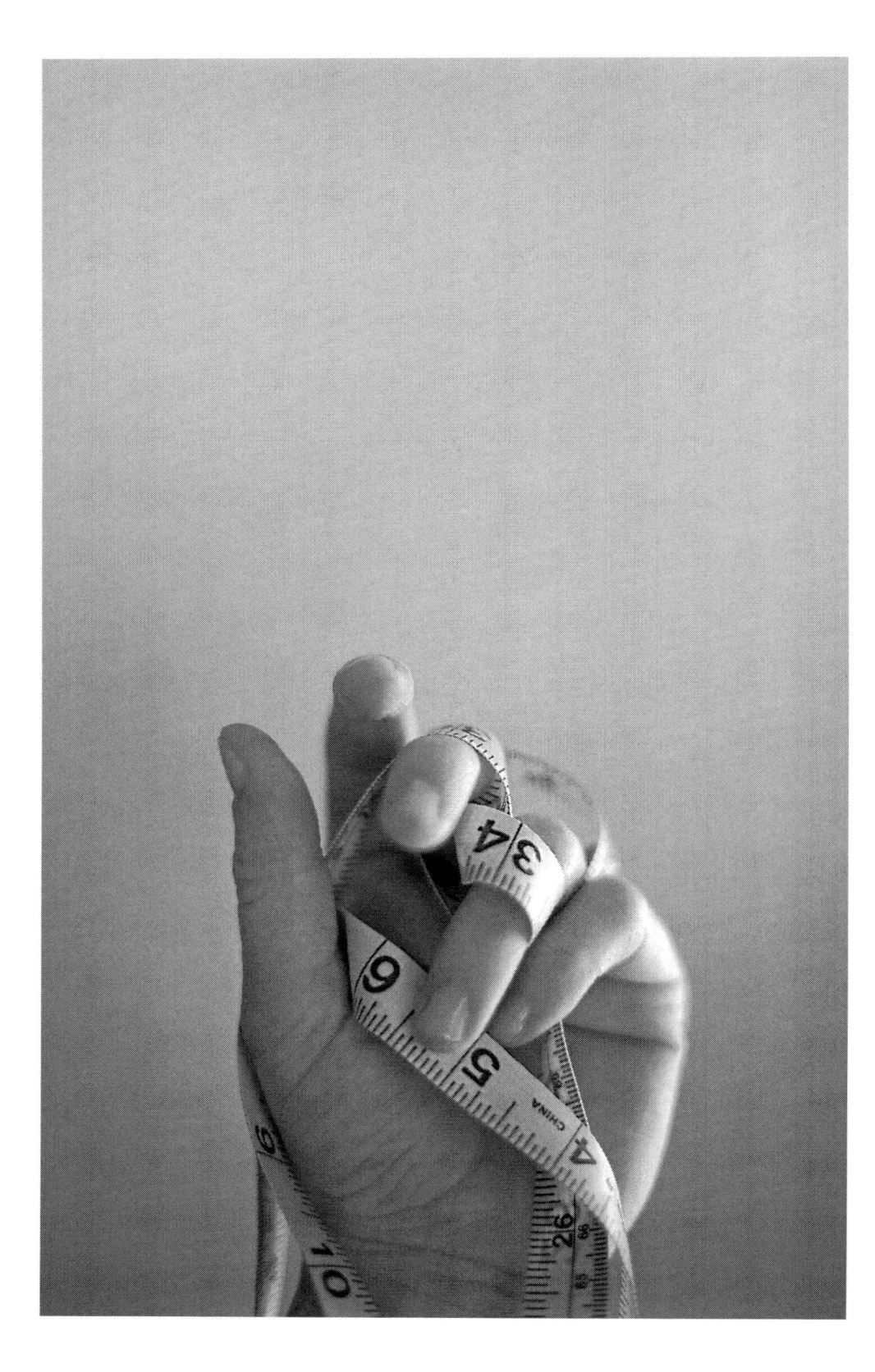

●

How much does she weigh? They ask, because
That's what people see when they're stuck in a
Myopic reality. When we open our eyes there's so
Much more to be instead of what's in magazines
Or being advertised on TV. She weighs a lifetime
Of superficial casualness that left some tears
And callouses when the truth is we shouldn't
Care about what she wears or whether anything
That involves her happiness does anything to
Diminish your personal cares. She weighs a
Lifetime of successes and failures that don't
Mean anything other than she tried, which is
Probably more than what anyone ever did that
Tried to strip her down and judge her by size.
She weighs the sum of so much more than what you
Could put on a scale, and see that's where
Society fails. She weighs life in moments and
Not in pounds and that's why she's the happiest
Girl around

● ● ●
Broken Footprints Faded Hearts

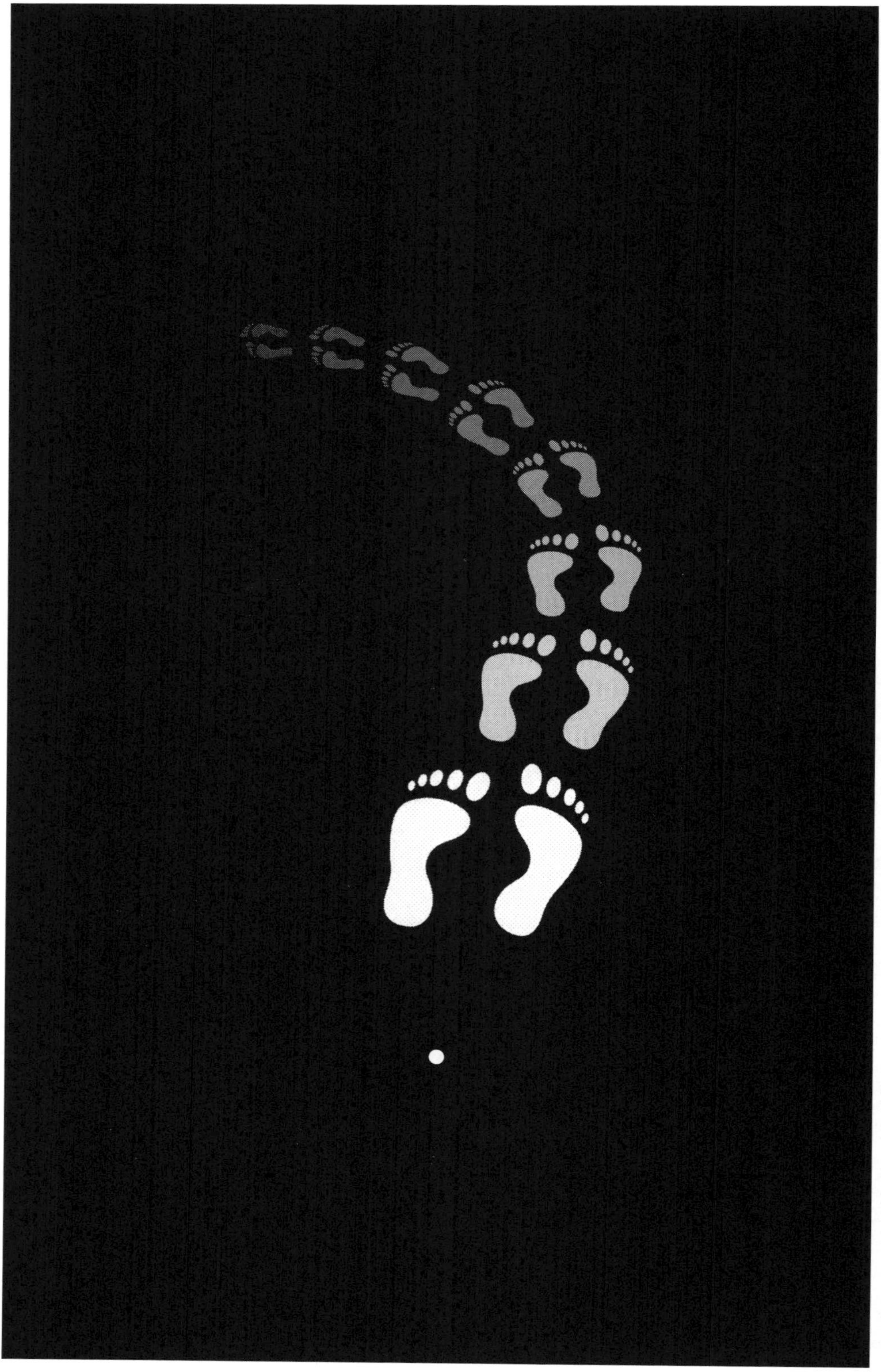

A real man will celebrate your
Strength, not fear it nor compete
With it. He will admire you for being
Strong and he'll be stronger for it too.
And the world you build together
Will be made of tougher stuff than the
One where weak souls sabotage you
With whispers of "not enough"

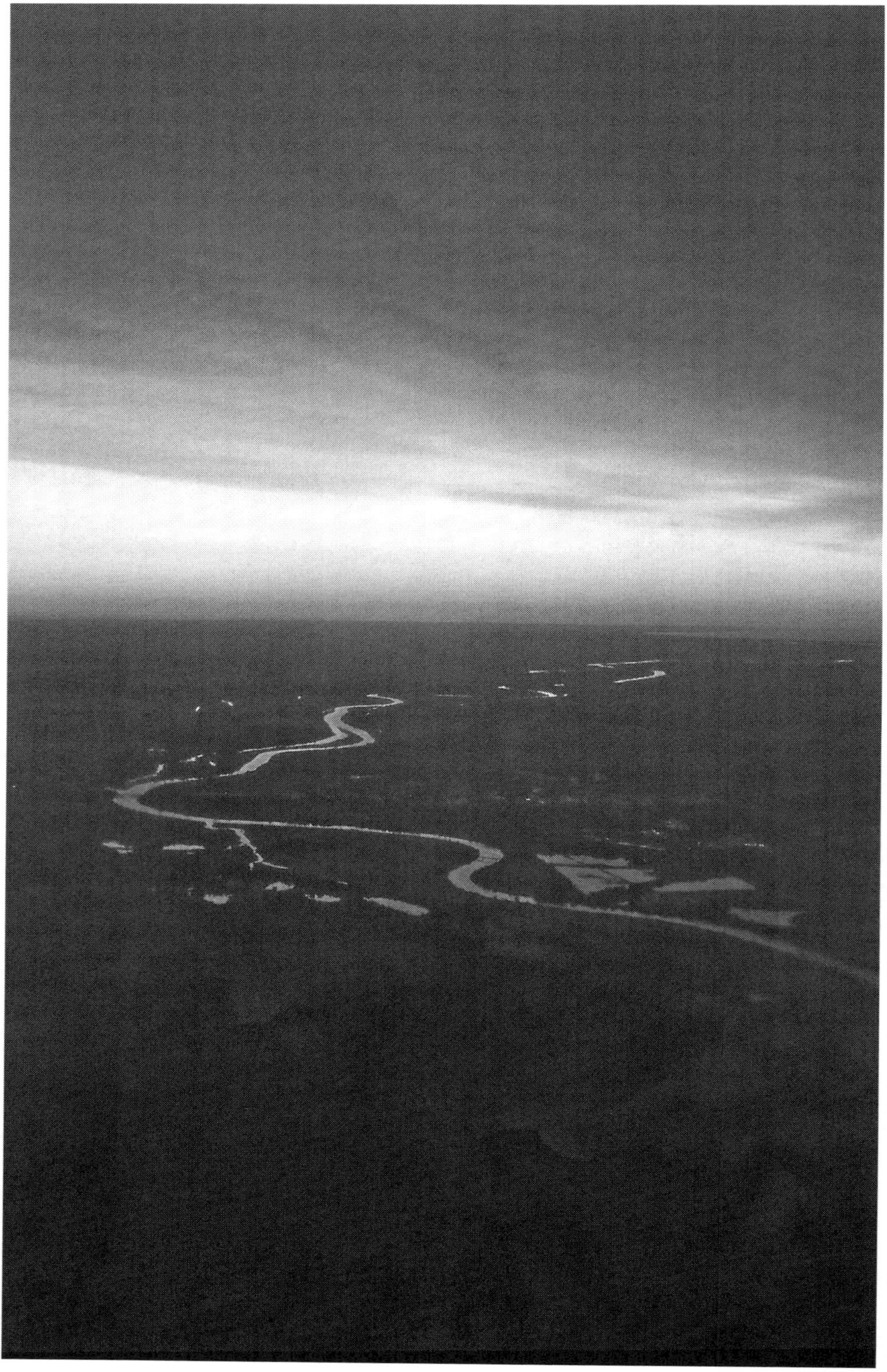

●

You want her to believe in your love,

To believe the words you say?

Just remember that people believe

In beautiful sunsets

Because they happen every day

• • •
Broken Footprints Faded Hearts

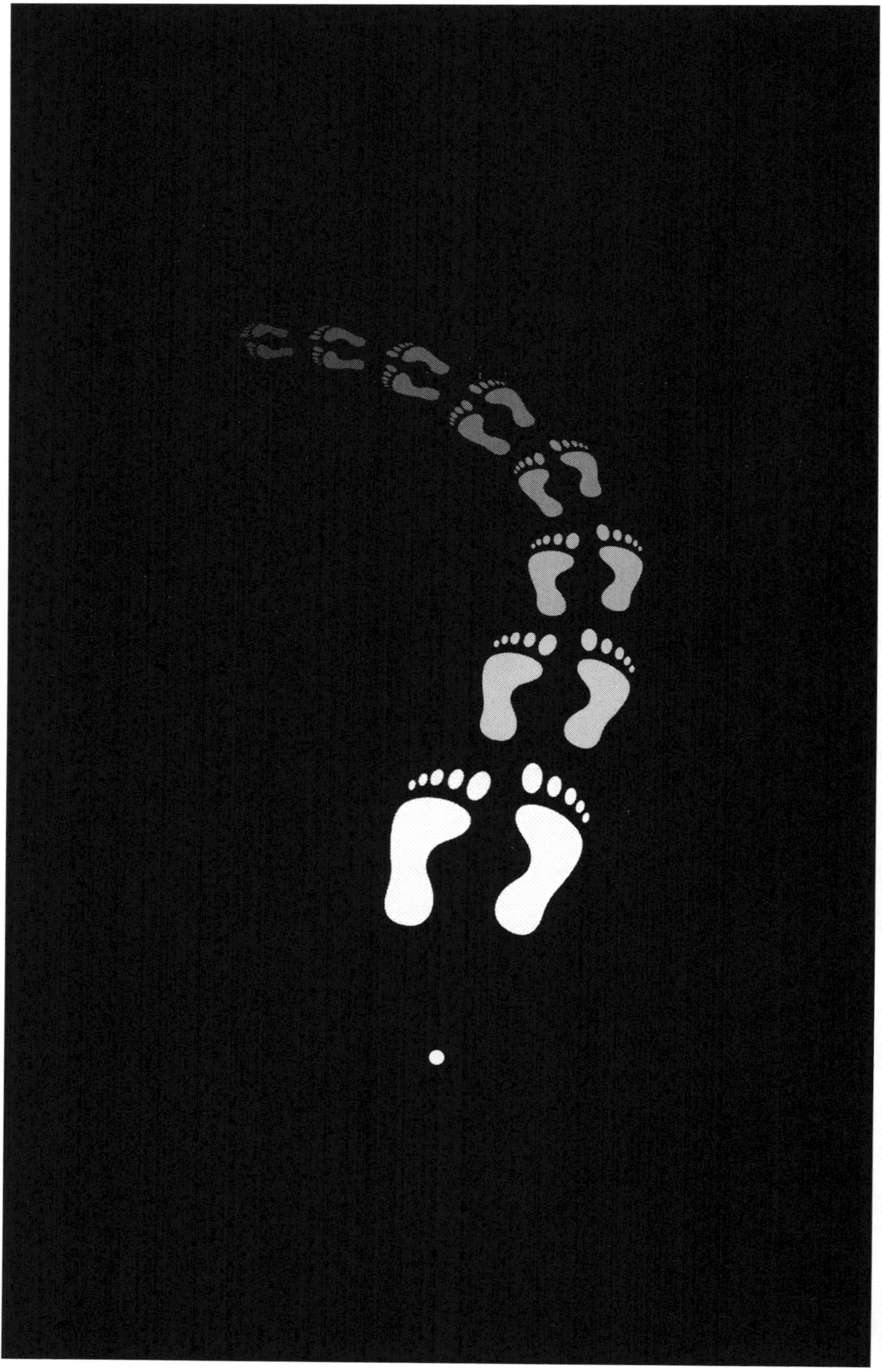

Real relationships

Don't revolve

Around perfection.

But you can get

Pretty far by

Being consistent

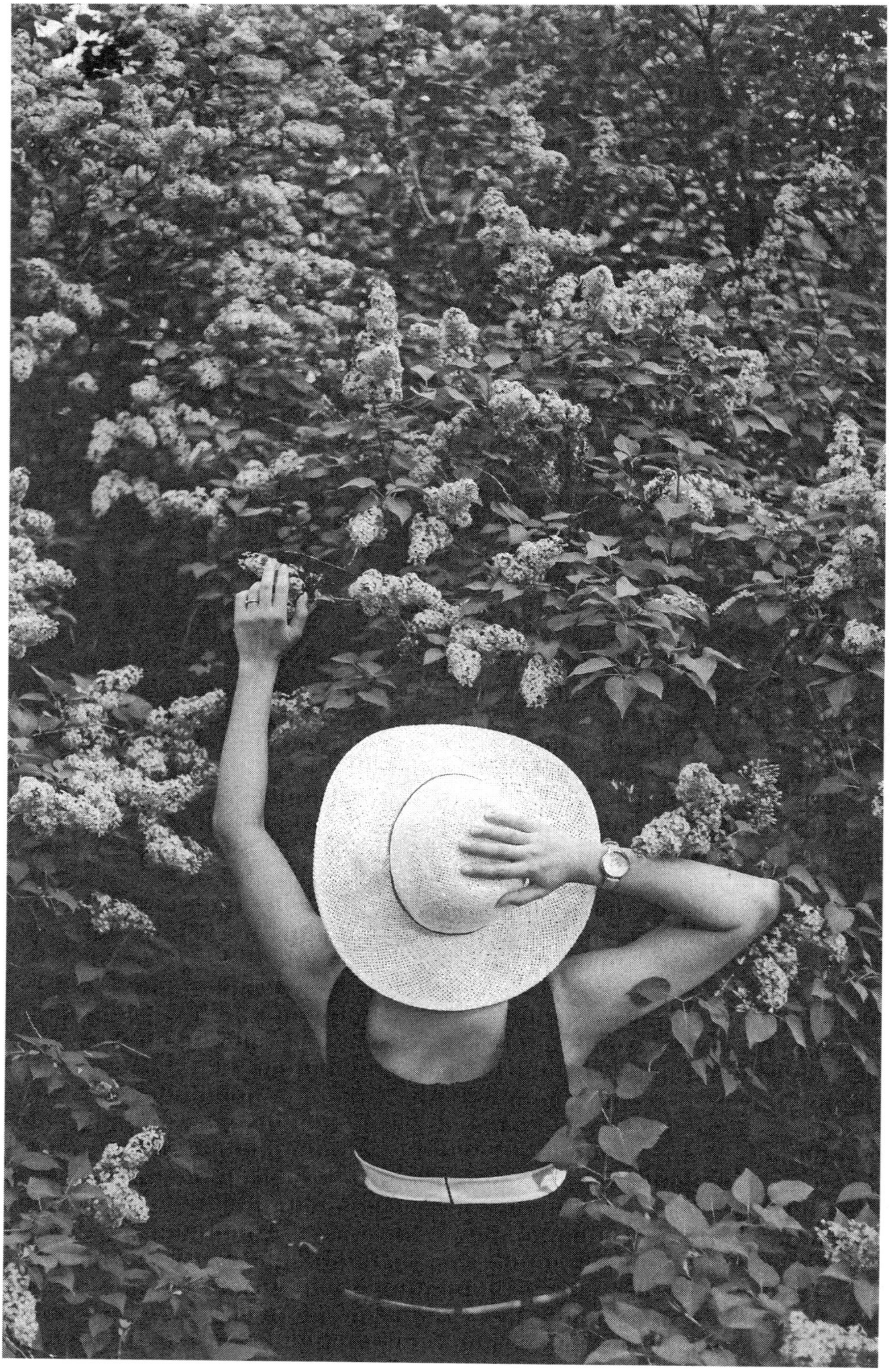

●

She braided lilacs in her hair,

A small reminder of fingers

That once played there

That not all that is

Beautiful shall last,

But there is beauty still

In moments past

• • •
Broken Footprints Faded Hearts

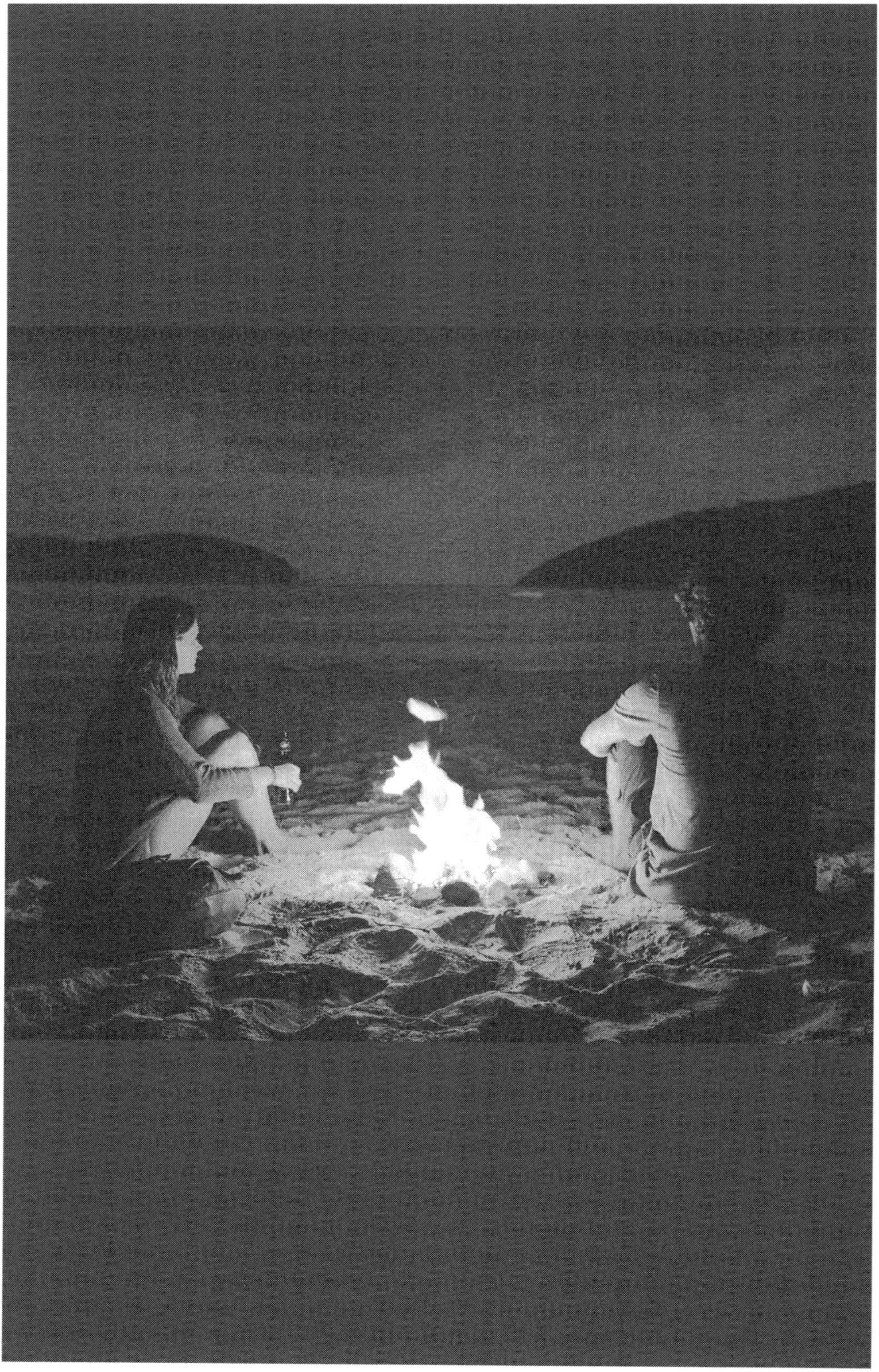

●

Two lovers beneath the starlit sky,

Know not the how or why.

May twin hearts find solace in four eyes.

Be brave, new love, in remembrance

Of the soldier's creed.

Lovers too must sacrifice and bleed.

For in all wars, souls are lost

But too victory may well be worth the cost.

And so, in love be brave

For we must shed the why

And together, do and die

● ● ●
Broken Footprints Faded Hearts

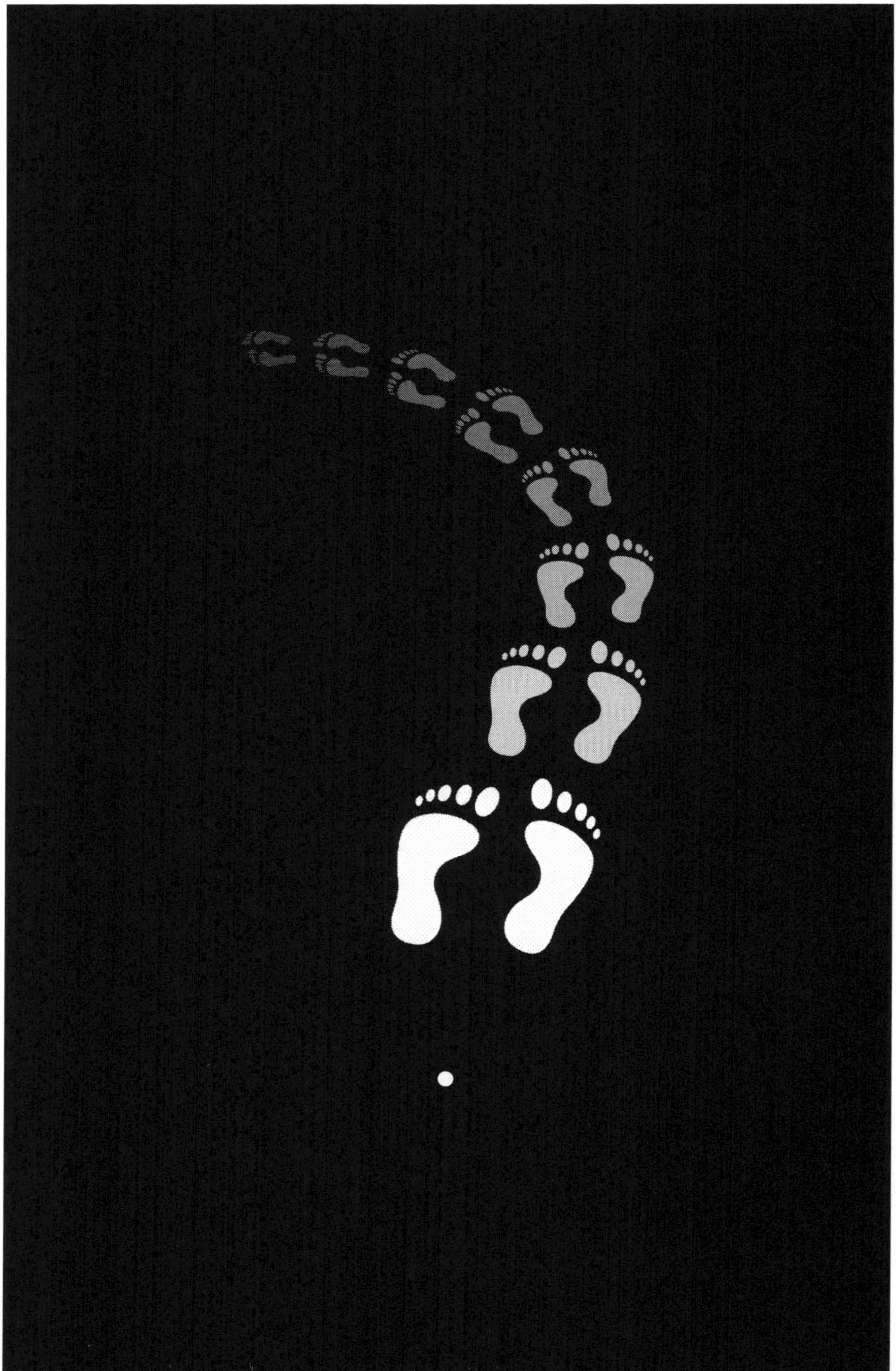

•

The problem with love is

People assign it mythical dimensions.

Mountains are majestic but ultimately

Made from dirt and rocks. Love is

Ninety percent being a rock in a world

Of dirt. That is the real optical illusion

Of love and just being a rock is its

Very plain and practical magic

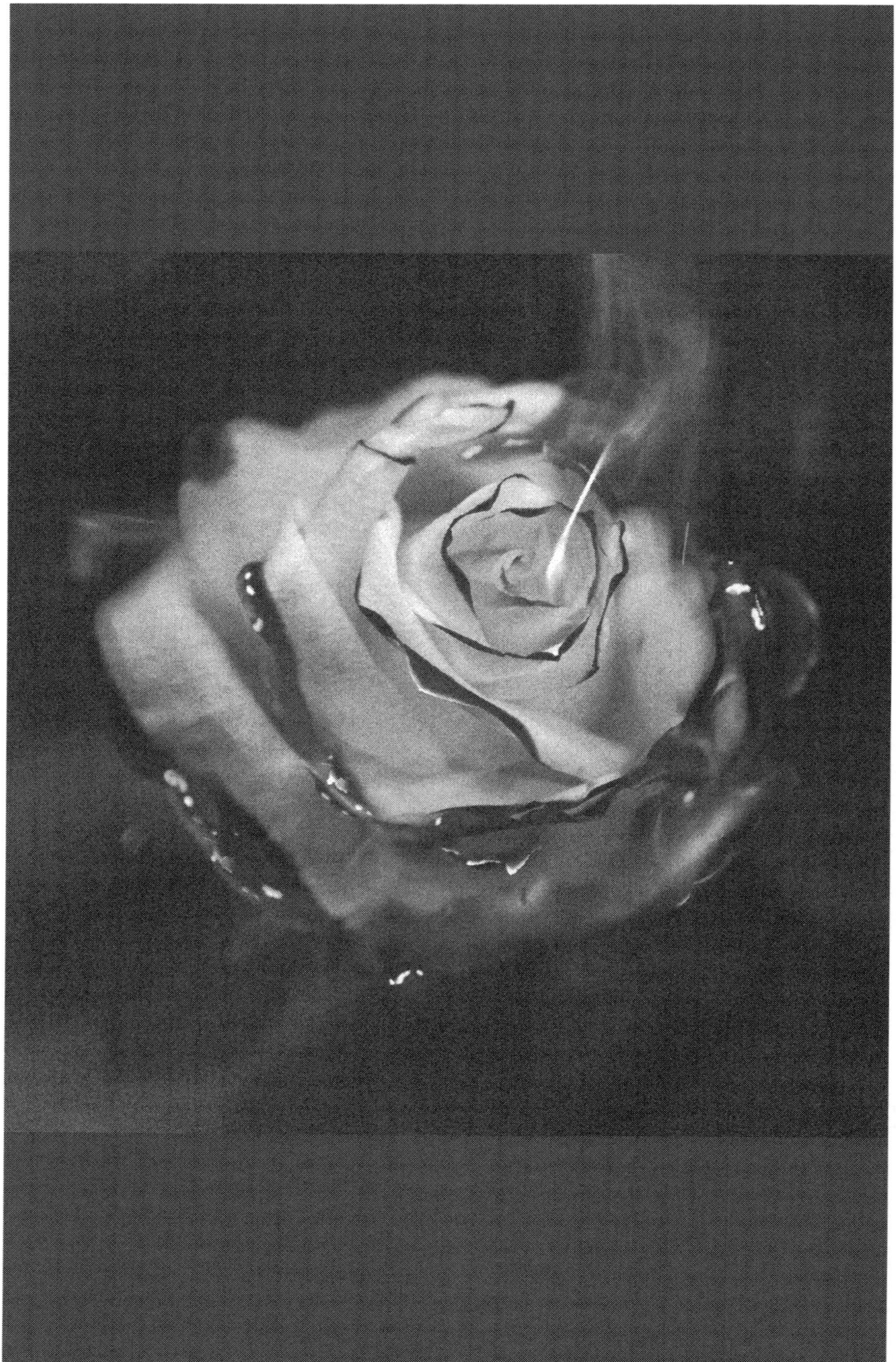

•

Sure, love can creep up on us slow and steady.
But sometimes it comes up on us like a fireball
On the back of a tornado. And that's okay. It's
Okay to let love give you whiplash while lighting
The sky on fire before falling out of the atmosphere
In a billion shattered embers. Because here's the
Secret champ, not everyone gets to ride on the back
Of a flaming tornado in their lifetime. But for your
Sake, I hope you do. Yeah, it's dangerous, but it's
A hell of a ride. Trust me. Lasso a tornado

•••
Broken Footprints Faded Hearts

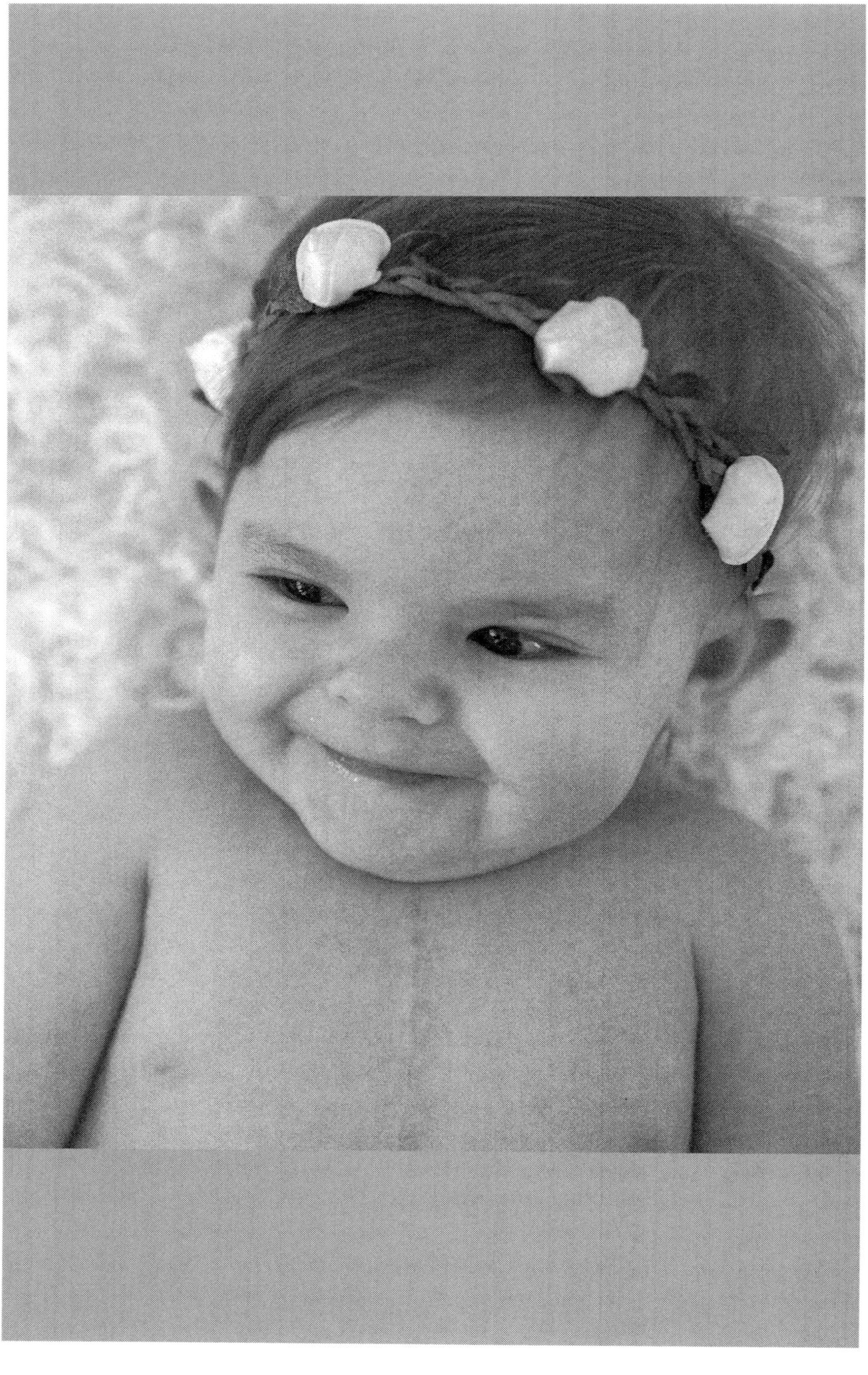

•

She bore a scar

Just above her lip

Because some god

Made her perfect

And in his jealousy

Let the chisel slip

You don't deserve her

Nobody deserves another

Person.

They earn them

Repeatedly

•

She finally realized what she's gotta do.

With sad eyes, she moves right through you.

There's a fire in her heart even you can't put out.

Call her crazy but she knows what she's about

And where you've ended was just supposed

To be the start.

And lately, she's been a whole in a thing where

She was promised to only play a part.

So, she's gotta do what a girl's gotta do,

And she goes on.

This ain't nothing new.

Just now, it's without you

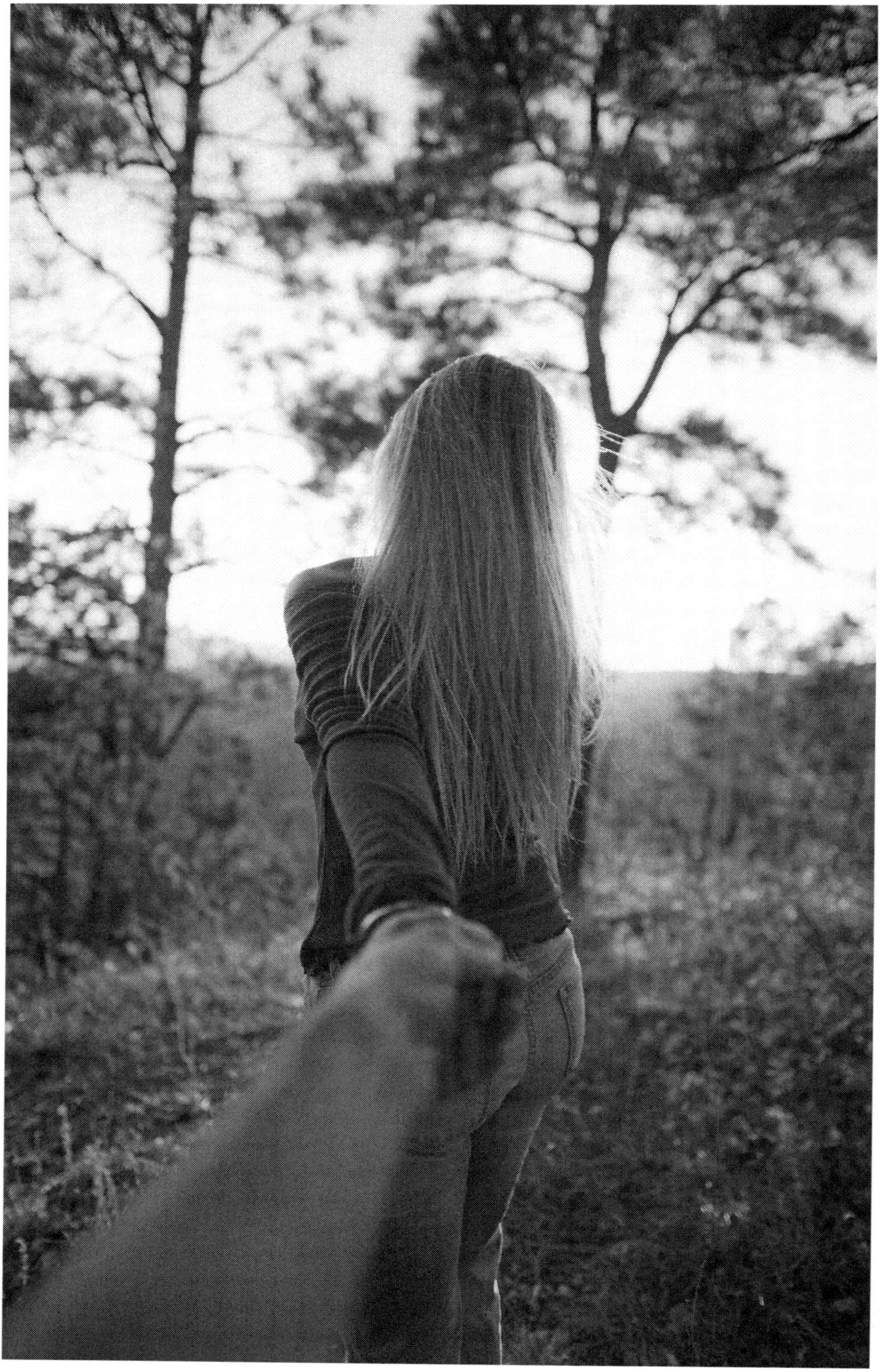

•

She found me

Broken and used –

Pieces of herself to

Build me back again.

And though still

I carry cracks,

I hold so much more love

Than when we first began

• • •
Broken Footprints Faded Hearts

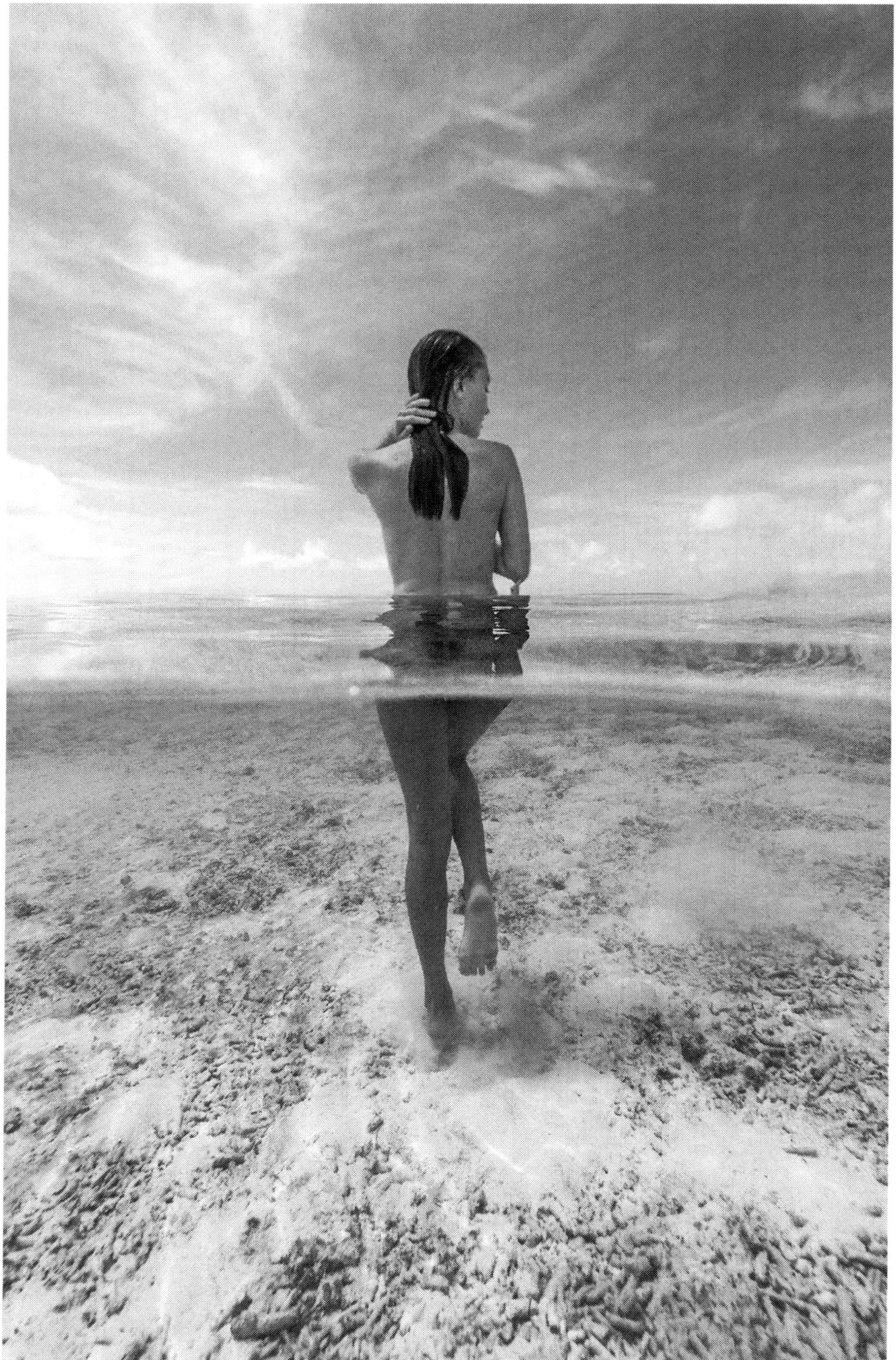

•

She danced naked on sand

To the rhythm of the sea.

She wore only moonlight

And a pair of helpless eyes.

Perfectly, she conducted

Such sorcery over me

• • •
Broken Footprints Faded Hearts

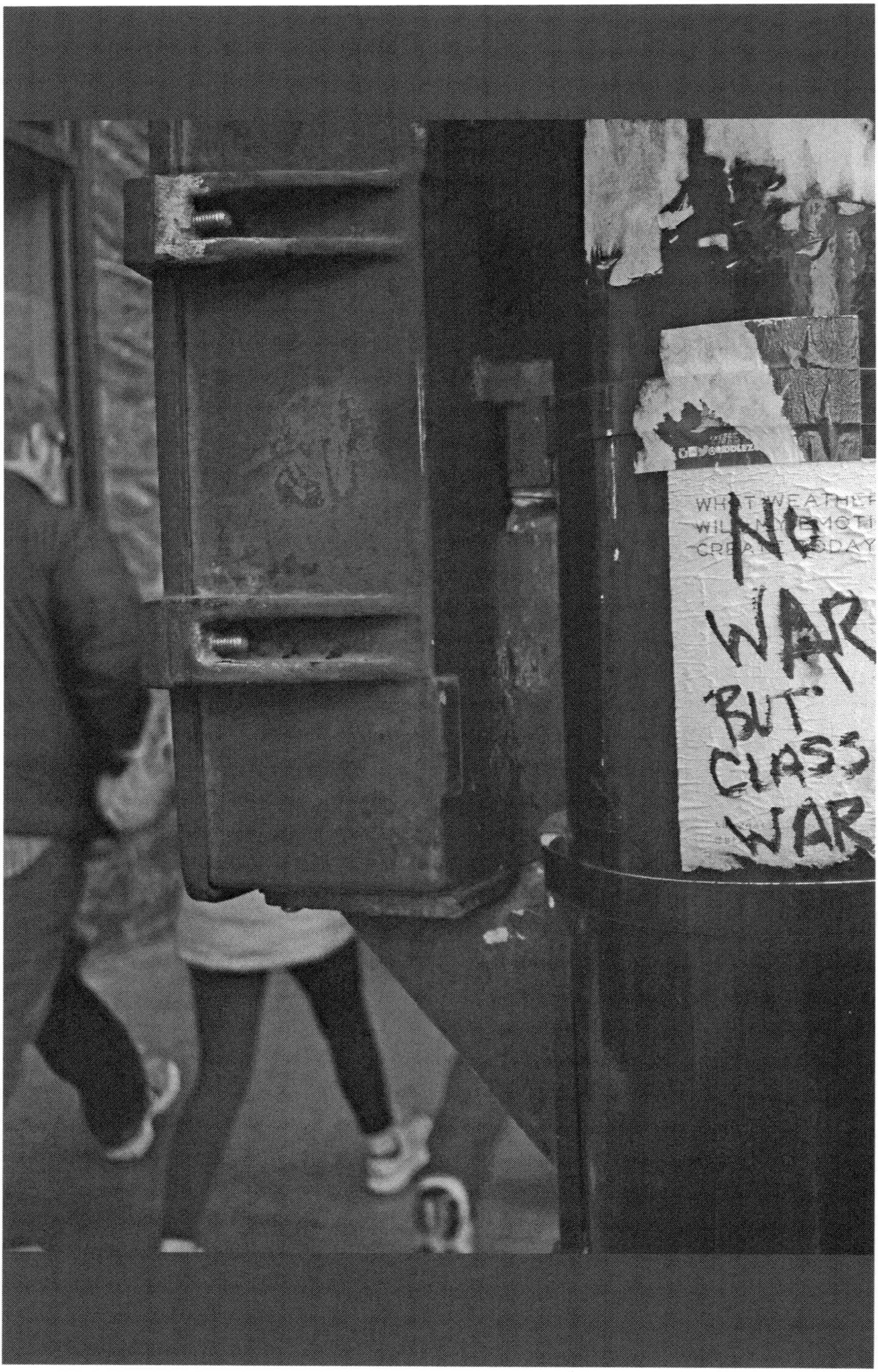
NO WAR BUT CLASS WAR

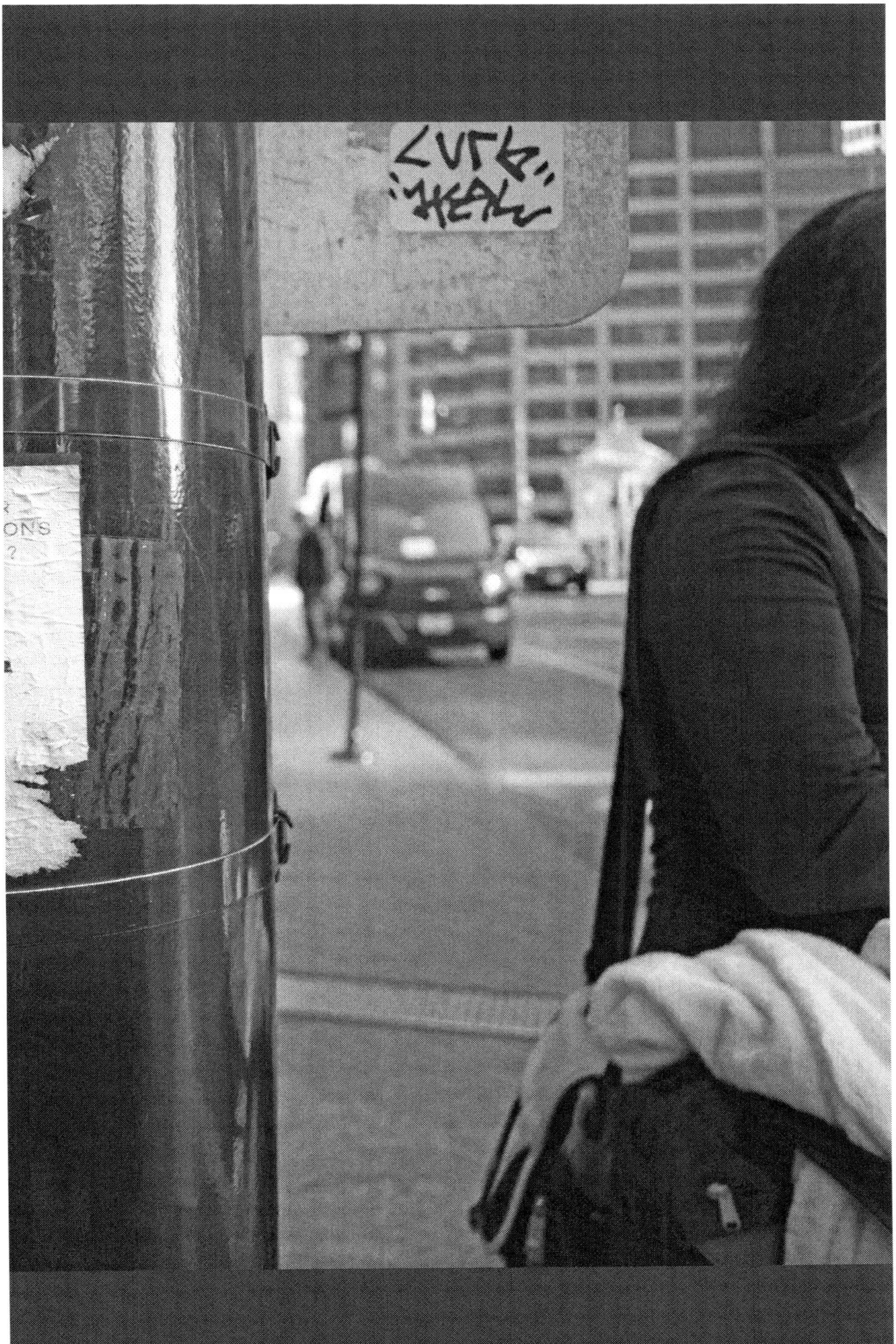

•

Tonight, I'm angry. I'm angry
    cuz I'm seeing these unchecked

Fires raging all around me. I'm angry
    cuz of this trash politicians

Are talking about on TV. I'm angry
    because these people, these

Women, close to me have to talk
    about #MeToo twenty years

Later, cuz for ages they thought there was
    nothing else they could do.

I'm angry. Maybe cuz all the shouting
    makes me feel I have to be.

I'm angry, maybe cuz of that word
    I always preach on called empathy

n.a.denmon

I'm angry. And I'm tired of that shit living
        inside of me but I'm angry.

And I feel like we can quelch these fires,
        and silence the political

Hypocrisy, and let these women live free,
        and be okay with these

Movements even if we don't all agree
        because we practice that empathy

And if I had you with me, I know we'd
        roll over this shit like a rolling sea

And maybe, just maybe, I could rest.
        And let go. And stop being angry.

And just be me

• • •

Broken Footprints Faded Hearts

●

You cannot make a thing of her
And expect her to still care for you.
Objects don't care at all.
Her spirit will object and demand
The personification which you
So casually deny.
And you'll' watch as the woman
Walks away, carrying all the things
You wanted, with her

She grew strong

Having suffered

The weaknesses

Of small men

Prone to inadequate

And cruel compensations

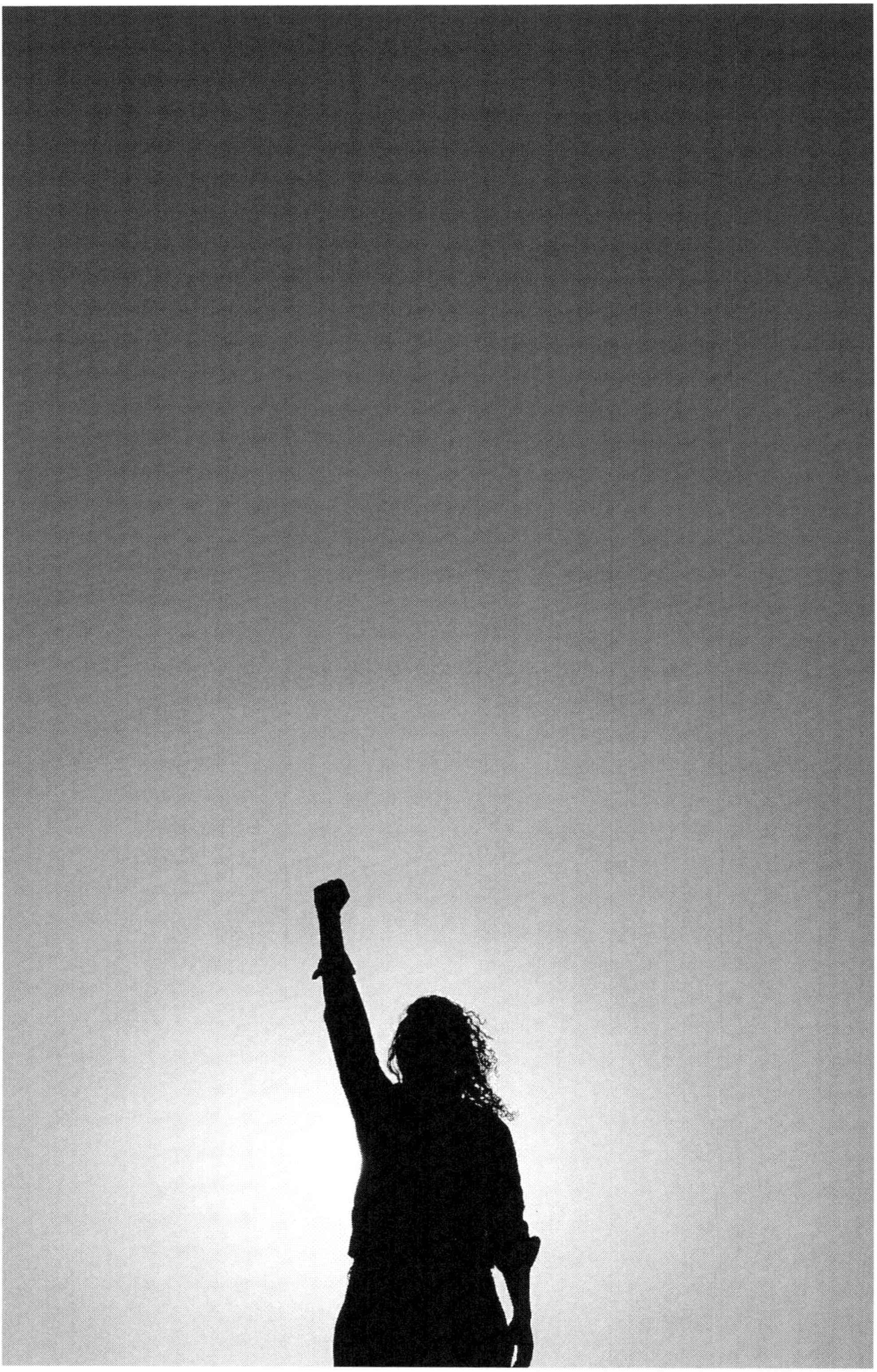

•

The most powerful thing
I've ever seen her do
Is put her pieces back
Together again with
No hands and no glue.
It's the simple necessary
Strength of those with
Hopeful and once-happy
Hearts, broken into two

• • •
Broken Footprints Faded Hearts

## About the Author

Nicholas Denmon was born in Buffalo, NY. He started storytelling from the moment he could talk and has spent a lifetime perfecting the art. Later, he studied English at the University of Florida. He is an accomplished novelist, poet, and also writes for The Huffington Post and several online magazines.

His life has been varied, giving him no shortage of material. Some of his unique experiences include growing up with a lovable yet schizophrenic mother, having five brothers and sisters (of which he is the middle-younger child), a perfectionist father, a **peculiar** step-mother, a college life of epic proportions, and working for politicians on the Presidential as well as the local stage. He has been, at times, a devout Catholic, a closet atheist, and an honorary member of the Jewish tribe.

Nick's joy of art knows little in the way of limitations, as he loves unique paintings, music, acting, film, and of course writing.

• • •
n.a.denmon

Made in the USA
Middletown, DE
31 January 2020